"An uplifting message full of positivity, life advice, possibility for change, and ideas to consider. An essential read for dreamers of all audiences."

-**Ebony Joy Wilkins**, author of
SELLOUT, SOMEONE TO HEAR ME,
and *THE WILL TO DANCE*

"Since my earliest memories as the son of a small town pastor I have been a dreamer. Those dreams allowed me to explore new worlds before my eyes actually saw them. In **So You Have a Dream . . . . Now What,** Michael L. Ford II shows us how those dreams can be affirmed by the wisdom of the scriptures and shaped into the future we want. Dream on . . . . and read on. You may be closer than you think to the life you've imagined."

-**Dan Miller**, bestselling author of
48 Days to the Work You Love

"Mr. Ford has synthesized many of the challenges that we all face as we travel along the journey toward dream fulfillment."

-**Desmon Daniel, Ph.D.**, author of
Giant Slayers

So, You Have a Dream... Now What?

It's time to get your head out of the clouds and make your dreams a reality!

By Michael Ford II

authorHOUSE®

AuthorHouse™
1663 Liberty Drive
Bloomington, IN 47403
www.authorhouse.com
Phone: 1-800-839-8640

First published by AuthorHouse 10/10/2011

ISBN: 978-1-4567-4221-8 (ebk)
ISBN: 978-1-4567-4222-5 (hc)
ISBN: 978-1-4567-4223-2 (sc)

Library of Congress Control Number: 2011902401

Printed in the United States of America

Table of Contents

Foreword

I sincerely believe that in the course of human events, everyone will be offered an opportunity to be a part of something great. Not only that, but every great thing that has happened has involved at least three elements. First, there was a void, a need, and an empty place to be filled. Second, there was a desire to meet that need, a push to make something happen, and an inspiration. Thirdly, there was action. Something was done.

It is this last element that makes me think of Michael Ford II more than the other two. When I first met Michael, there was no indication of his final status, just as even now, "it doth not yet appear…" There was, however, every indication that there was something great in him, just waiting to be released.

Michael comes from a good, solid, and stable family. His parents are examples of investors in human capital. His siblings are go-getters and successful. His wife is the perfect yin to Mike's yang. I watch his children grow and know that they possess the same potentials. But Mike's real strength is his ability to take action. It is that action that has produced this wonderful book.

As the scripture suggests, with strength, "Physician, heal thyself!" this book is a healing balm for Mike and his generation.

He is a part of a demographic that has lately been described as "The Millennials." This group will provide leadership for the next century, based on a set of beliefs that include making a difference in the lives of others, unselfish investment in the lives of others, and success that is not simply defined in dollars and cents.

This book will help every reader because it is an honest presentation of the soul of an inspired individual. I am proud to be a part of his life and destiny. I know that joining the journey toward success will enhance your life as well.

Pastor Hurley J. Coleman, Jr.
World Outreach Campus of Greater Coleman Temple Ministries
www.WorldOutreachCampus.org

Introduction

Are you a wide-awake dreamer? Do you find yourself dreaming while on the job? Dreaming while doing work around the house? Dreaming while walking through the mall? If your answer is "yes," to any of the questions above, you, my friend, are a wide-awake dreamer! And, this rare ability makes you a powerful person! Author T.E. Lawrence once said, *"All men dream but not equally. Those that dream by night in the dusty recesses of their minds wake in the day to find that it was vanity; but the dreamers of the day are dangerous men, for they may act their dream with open eyes to make it possible."* YOU ARE DANGEROUS!

Some may consider wide-awake dreaming a deficiency. I consider it a blessing as long as you know how to harness the power of being a dreamer and make the most of it. I have personally seen how dreaming during the day can cause problems. But, to try to completely squash your dreams during the time when your brain is most active, would be utterly absurd. As a wide-awake dreamer, you must begin to take hold of your dreams and work to see them become reality.

Let's face it; if you only dream of better days, and better things when you close your eyes to sleep, you are absolutely powerless to make them happen. But you, as a wide-awake dreamer, have the power to make your dreams come true simply because you allow yourself to dream during the day.

Don't allow your dreams to simply spoil in your mind. Instead, turn your dreams into well thought-out and deliberate actions, and you will begin to see through the mirror of your potential and realize that objects in your dreams are "closer than they appear."

First step; as wide-awake dreamers, we've got to learn to plan our days, and take advantage of our moments. Now, read chapter one, and let's figure this thing out together.

Chapter 1

Plan Your Day

A well-known, beloved, man of God passes away suddenly in the middle of the night. Several children are killed in a house fire. When tragedies like these happen, oftentimes we feel our own mortality more than ever. We recognize that life is not promised and that while today we live; tomorrow, we could be gone. As a matter of fact, the only moment of life that we truly own is the moment that we are living in right now. In the next second, if God does not provide us with another breath, it will be all over.

After reading those words, many people would say, "If life is so fragile, what's the sense in dreaming of better days ahead?" Indeed, life is not promised to us. However, because tomorrow is not a guarantee does not mean that we should forget about our dreams and concede to live a life of mediocrity. Actually, it's quite the contrary. Because life has no guarantees, we should be more concerned with living in our *moments*. Many times, we look at life in days, weeks, and years instead of moments. For the dreamer, this is a mistake. The dreamer must learn to take life one moment at a time.

If you've ever watched a ball game, undoubtedly, you've heard a broadcaster say something like, "The *momentum* has shifted to the home team with that huge play!" Momentum is something that can shift an entire game in the behalf of one team or the other; many times, based on one play. In a football game, all it takes is a timely interception. In a basketball game, it may only take a steal and a fast-break dunk that brings the home team crowd to their feet, and turns a close game into a blow-out. One play. One moment. All you need is one momentum-shifting play! One play can make all the difference!

Remember, it's all about the moments. When we take advantage of our moments, we begin to shift momentum in our favor. One immediate and deliberate change can be just the thing that you need to draw yourself closer to the success that you envision for your life.

In all actuality, if we don't take time to appreciate and make the most of our moments, we run the risk of eventually losing days, weeks, and years of progress.

Let's think about this a little closer. In a day there are;

24 *hours*

60 *minutes in every hour*

60 *seconds in every minute*

Nothing groundbreaking there right? I know. But sometimes we need to see things in good ole' black and white in order to put them in the proper perspective. Now, just for a little fun, let's add those numbers together; 24 + 60 + 60 = **144**. Now, let's take a look at **Psalms 144**. In the first verse King David writes, "Praise the LORD, who is my rock. *He trains my hands for war and gives* *my fingers skill for battle* (NLT; emphasis mine). How about that? King David acknowledges that it is God who gives him the skill and wherewithal to fight, but it is the King himself who has to engage in the battle. As a dreamer, we are in a direct conflict with the enemy. The enemy does not like people who have hope for a brighter future. He does not like dreamers. Therefore, as dreamers, we have to be prepared to engage in the fight for our dreams every day. Many people have quoted the verse in the book of Numbers, chapter 20; "the battle is not ours, it's the Lord's." But, while God will most certainly defend us, we must not take this verse to mean that we can sit back with our arms folded and watch God handle all of our business for us. God forbid. We must become a part of the battle. We must do what we can do, and after we have done all that we can, we can trust God to bring about the victory.

We serve an awesome God, but that does not give us an excuse to be lazy. There are twenty-four hours in each day. How can we say that we don't have enough time?

For many of us, I don't believe the problem is that we don't have enough time. Instead, we are just not using our time effectively. Let me ask you this; do you participate in fantasy sports? Why do I ask? Well, I recently read an article that stated that avid fantasy sport players average nine business hours a week claiming players off the waiver wire, fixing their lineups, making trades, and doing other things concerning their fantasy team. Nine hours a week may not seem like a lot, but it's like working another full days worth of work! If you are a fantasy sport player, and you are one of those guys that come home from work and instantly jump on the computer to check your fantasy team every day, you have to consider whether or not some of your time is being wasted. You have to *aggressively* take back your time. Key word: aggressively. Taking your time back is not one of those things that will necessarily come easy.

So, how do we make the most of our moments and maximize our time? I believe the answer is found in scheduling.

Every day is filled with opportunities. When we wake up in the morning, it is our responsibility to decide how we are going to use the time that each day provides. Have you ever felt like there just isn't enough time in the day to do the things that you want to do? I mean, you have children to attend to, a spouse that needs your time, jobs, church responsibilities, and community service. You may be wondering, "Where do I find time to work on fulfilling my dreams?"

Over the last few years, I have found that it is important to schedule time in your day that is specifically delegated to *dream pursuit*. If we don't intentionally schedule time in our day to work on our dreams, we won't find the time. Time for dream pursuit will not present itself to you. If you're waiting for time to come up to you, tap you on the shoulder and say, "Here I am, use me," you are sadly mistaken. It's not going to happen. This is where the aggression comes in; you have to master your time. You have to tell your time what to do.

Consider this; twenty-four hours can be divided in a lot of ways. Let's just say that your job takes up eight hours of each weekday. That still leaves you with sixteen hours in each day. Now, do you really need eight hours of sleep every night? If you do, then you're still left with eight hours. Even if those last 8 hours are packed with church, homework, and family responsibilities, you owe it to yourself to take out at least one hour each day to work on your small business, write a page of your book, or look up information on the internet. Remember, your dream is your responsibility. While others may be there to tell you, "You can do it!" – No one is going to work to make your dream come true except you! And, it *does* take work! The sad truth about men is this; too many of us have tremendous dreams of success, but we really don't want to work!

Some of you may still be thinking to yourself, "I hear what you're saying, but my days are just too busy." I beg to differ. People generally find time to do the things that they want to do. For me, playing video games is more of an enjoyable recreation than fantasy football. I can sit in front of my TV playing games for hours straight (and I have done it). Even on some of my busiest days, I've found time to play video games for at least an hour. What does that say about me; besides the fact that I'm a kid at heart? It says that on those days, I made video games a *priority*. If I make video games a priority every day and neglect the pursuit of my dreams, whose fault is it when I remain on chapter one of a book for three years, or my business never takes off? It's mine.

Let's take a closer look at this word; *priority*. Webster's dictionary gives several great definitions of this word, but there is one definition that I would like to focus on: *"something given or meriting attention before competing alternatives."* The first part of this statement that sticks out for me is, "competing alternatives." Every single day, our attention, focus, time, and motivation has to be divided amongst competing alternatives. There are always options! Ultimately, the choice is yours. What will you make time for today? This is a question that you have to answer bright and early in the morning. As soon as your alarm clock goes off and your feet hit the floor, you have to decide which competing alternatives you are going to give your attention to. The definition clearly states that some things actually merit attention while other things are merely given attention unworthily.

Everything is competing for your time. Some of the things are very necessary. Others are not. What can you do without in order to make progress toward your dream? Is it really necessary to go to the gym every day? Would it kill you to take a night off from your bowling league? Do you have to watch television for three hours a day?

Your day is full of opportunity. The pursuit of your dream has to be a priority for you. If it's not a priority, you can forget about it coming true. Even as I wrote that last line, I started to think. Often times, people miss out on their dreams because they believe that dreams just *come true*. While that is an accurate statement—dreams do come true—I really think there should be a disclaimer that goes along with it: *"If you are willing to work very hard at it."* Many times people are quick to tell us that anything is possible, but they neglect to tell us that it will take hard work and sacrifice in order for our dreams to become a reality. So, if someone were to monitor your day and take an inventory of how you spend your time, what would they see as your highest priorities? All of us have a number of priorities in our lives; God, family, work, school, and recreation, for instance. The challenge is to put them all in the right order. Because our moments matter so much; in chapter two, let's take a look at some challenges to making the pursuit of our dreams a top priority.

Chapter 2

Hurdles to Dream Pursuit

First of all, let me say this; you have already jumped over one of the biggest hurdles there is. You have a dream! Believe it or not, there are so many men in this world who have no dreams, nor hope for tomorrow. So, you are already off to a great start.

There are more challenges to making dream pursuit a priority than I can possibly cover in one chapter, but I want to talk about a few of them. In my own life, I have noticed that one of my hurdles is *guilt*. I feel guilty spending time pursuing my dream because there are always other things that need to be done. The house needs to be cleaned, several home improvement jobs are undone, the car needs to go to the shop, and the kids have extra-curricular activities that they have to attend. Why would I take time out of a busy day just to work on something that is not guaranteed to succeed? The answer is simple; you owe it to yourself. Besides, how many things in life are guarantees? If you continually put off the pursuit of your dream, when will you ever find time? Who else is going to have to deal with the regret and remorse later in life, when you realize you did not make dream pursuit a priority?

YOU DO NOT HAVE TO FEEL GUILTY FOR TAKING TIME TO PURSUE YOUR DREAMS.

Go ahead, take a moment and tell yourself, "I do not have to feel guilty for taking time to pursue my dreams." Now, with that being said, it's very obvious that some of the things that I mentioned earlier cannot be put off forever. But realistically, you can't clean the house, fix the car, and complete your whole list of home improvement jobs in one day. So, why not plug in some time for dream pursuit today?

You cannot afford to miss the moment. Take advantage of now. Take advantage of *this* day. There are things that can be done in this moment and on this day that cannot be done on any other day. I've often heard the quote, "Yesterday is gone, tomorrow is not promised, today is a gift; that's why it's called the present." The psalmist says it like this in Psalms 118:24; "*This is the day* that the Lord hath made, let us rejoice and be glad in it." (emphasis mine). The author of this verse was making a point to do what he enjoys *today*, not tomorrow or next week. Think about it this way: this day, the very day that you have taken a few moments to read this book, is the only day that you have. To wait until tomorrow to do what you can do today is absurd. If you desire to leave a legacy that matters, you must start today; which leads me to the next hurdle to dream pursuit: *procrastination*.

Proverbs 6:4 says, "*Don't put it off; do it now! Don't rest until you do.*" It's really simple; dreamers cannot afford to be procrastinators. Well, let me say it like this; dreamers, who have any desire to see their dreams become a reality, cannot be procrastinators. If you want to be the type of person who talks about their dreams, thinks about their dreams, even dreams about their dreams, but never puts anything into motion, then yes, you can procrastinate. But, if you are one of those dreamers who really want to see some things happen, you have to rid yourself of the urge to procrastinate. *Wikipedia.com* defines procrastination as *"the counterproductive deferment of actions or tasks to a later time."* There are some things that you can do as a wide-awake dreamer that will slow you down in your efforts to pursue your dreams; and those things are bad enough. Procrastination is worse. Not only does procrastination slow down your progress, but because it is counterproductive, it actually produces problems of its own. When you start procrastinating about things, it will not be long before procrastination becomes a habitual part of your life, and as we all know, habits can be extremely hard to break. My advice to you is this; avoid the hassle. Confront your temptation to procrastinate *today.*

I was watching a pro football game on television a few days ago, and I noticed something. Many times, a sense of *urgency* is essential to success. I had been watching the game for a couple of hours, and the away team had struggled to move the ball up and down the field. However, with the score being 28-17 with only a little over five minutes remaining, the away team scored two touchdowns in a matter of three minutes and ended up winning the game 34-28. Having their backs up against the wall and realizing they didn't have much time caused them to do away with their usual pace, and instead, they began to use a no-huddle offense. Their sense of urgency proved to be just what they needed to win. Are you urgent in your dream pursuit? Or, are you taking a weak, "I'll do it tomorrow" stance?

Many times, procrastination is a by-product of fear. Fear of the unknown. Fear of failure. My pastor always says, "The one thing that you can be sure that you have never failed at is something that you have never tried." So, whatever your dream is, isn't it worth trying? You have to understand that failure is simply a part of success. It is inevitable that you will have some failures on your way to success. So, get over it! The old saying goes, "If at first you don't succeed, try, try, again."

When you feel the drive to begin work on dream pursuit and the next thought that enters your mind is, "but what if it's a waste of time?" or "what if you fail and everyone knows?" you have to recognize the source. The enemy of your peace, the devil himself, is the author of such things. He will always try to build up a spirit of fear in the hearts and minds of God's people; especially men. As the head of our households, if the enemy can cripple us with fear, and hinder our hope for tomorrow, he can seriously damage our family outlook. For the sake of our families, we must rebuke him, and continue to hold on to our dreams. For II Timothy 1:7 says, "God hath not given us the spirit of **fear**; but of power, and of love, and of a sound mind." Fear of this kind does not come from God. God wants us to pursue the desires of our heart. He wants us to prosper. You don't believe me? Read III John 1:2. It says, "Beloved, I wish above all things that thou mayest prosper and be in health, even as thy soul prospereth." It is God's desire that we first prosper in spiritual things, but I also believe that he wants us to prosper in the pursuit of our dreams and the desires of our hearts as well.

Prosperity is on the horizon! It's time to do our part to reach the heights that God has planned for us!

As I mentioned above, fear of failure is something that many people deal with. It's easy to feel this way especially when you are attempting to do something that no one around you has ever done. Again I say; failure is a natural part of success. Can you imagine how many times Benjamin Franklin must have failed before he figured out that he could harness the power of lightning to create electricity? What about Alexander Graham Bell and the telephone? The Wright Brothers and the airplane? I'm sure they all had their fair share of failures before reaching ultimate success. We have to come to grips with the fact that failure does not mean we failed completely. It simply means we had a minor setback. Failure is only a stumbling block on the road to success. The only people who don't trip over it are those who don't attempt to do anything.

Read II Timothy 1:7 again. It says, "God has not given us the *spirit* of fear." This verse lets us know that fear is a spirit. Therefore, we must recognize, early, that we cannot fight a spiritual battle with carnal, fleshly, weapons. It just won't work. We will discourage ourselves if we persist to try to fight with the wrong weapons. Spiritual warfare can only be fought using spiritual weapons. II Corinthians 10:4 informs us *that "the weapons of our warfare are not carnal, but mighty through God to the pulling down of strong holds; Casting down imaginations, and every high thing that exalteth itself against the knowledge of God, and bringing into captivity every thought to the obedience of Christ."* When you wake up in the morning with a powerful drive to push toward the fulfillment and manifestation of your dreams, don't let the devil rob you of that passion! As soon as the negative thoughts enter your mind, take hold of them! Don't allow those thoughts to float around in your mind and grow into a wall of fear and anxiety .You have the power to bring those thoughts into captivity and cast them out of your mind. Don't sit there and let the devil have his way in your psyche. When a thought enters your mind that is contrary to the Word of God, you know it can't be from God, so take hold of it and cast it out immediately! Believe it or not, you have that much power!

Prayer, fasting, and speaking the Word to the enemy of our minds is the only way to render him useless and powerless to defeat us in the pursuit of our dreams. Ephesians 6 informs us that we must put on the "whole armor" of God if we want to be able to stand against the enemy. We need the *protection of power* that the armor of God provides for us if we want to be able to rebuff the devices of the enemy. Let's take a closer look at Ephesians chapter 6, and try to get an understanding of what the armor of God entails. I have taken the liberty to highlight what I believe to be a few of the key words in these next few verses;

> [10]*Finally, my brethren, be strong in the Lord,*
> *and in the power of his might.*
> [11]*Put on the **whole** armour of God, that ye may be*
> *able to stand against the wiles of the devil.*
> [12]*For we wrestle not against flesh and blood, but against*
> *principalities, against powers, against the rulers of the darkness*
> *of this world, against spiritual wickedness in high places.*
> [13]*Wherefore take unto you the whole armour of God, that ye may*
> *be able to withstand in the evil day, and having done all, to stand.*

*[14]Stand therefore, having your loins girt about with **truth**,*
*and having on the breastplate of **righteousness**;*
*[15]And your feet shod with the **preparation of the gospel of peace**;*
*[16]Above all, taking the **shield of faith**, wherewith ye shall*
be able to quench all the fiery darts of the wicked.
*[17]And take the **helmet of salvation**, and the **sword***
*of the Spirit**, which is the word of God:*
*[18]**Praying** always with all prayer and supplication*
in the Spirit, and watching thereunto with all
perseverance and supplication for all saints."

The first word that I want to talk about is, "*whole.*" The author of these verses has laid out an entire body of armor that we can use to stand against the enemy of our peace, and the destroyer of our drive to succeed. By using the word, "whole," I think it is made very clear that we must endeavor to equip ourselves with every part of the armor of God. We cannot afford to neglect any piece. Every piece of the armor gives us a specific protection and power, and in our everyday fight for our dreams, we need every part of God's armor. I'm not going to try to explain every piece of the armor here, but as wide-awake dreamers, we must: study the Word of God to know the *truth*, have a heart that is bent toward honoring Christ, prepare our minds for spiritual battle daily, equip ourselves with faith no matter how insurmountable the task may seem, remember the sacrifice of our Savior at all times, and rely on the strength of the Word to give us peace and a hope for a better tomorrow. Lastly, the author reminds us to pray. We must not only pray for ourselves and our families, but we must also pray for others. You aren't the only one who has a dream. Pray for the success of your neighbor's company. Pray for your pastor. Spend time in intercessory prayer. You will find that there is peace in allowing God to use you in this way.

Another hurdle to dream pursuit is *laziness*. This one is simple. If you spend too much time sitting around or lying in bed, it's rather difficult to progress in the pursuit of your dreams. So, I say this with all due respect; GET UP! That dream that you have in your heart will not be fulfilled as long as you are sitting on the sidelines. Your dreams need your participation. So, get up and stop making excuses!

Laziness is one of those hurdles that really hits close to home for me. I really enjoy sleeping! What can I say? It's just really enjoyable. But, if you know you have the potential to be a lazy person, you have to be honest with yourself and admit the fact that you are what you are, and decide to make the necessary changes. You're not going to make anything happen lying on your back. Laziness is a hurdle that requires you to face the music and make changes **immediately**. Because of the severity of some challenges, it's best to make a move right away. Don't wait! Take the initial fire that you feel when the motivation for dream pursuit is at its highest peak, and use it to your advantage. We've all heard the saying, "If you snooze, you lose." Well, it's true. Don't allow that snooze button to rob you of time that you need for dream pursuit.

Instead of sleeping in because it's Saturday, get up early anyhow. Find something to do. Even if you don't necessarily work on your dream every Saturday, get up early anyway. Change is very rarely easy, so at first you may find that your body just doesn't like getting up early, especially when you don't have to. You may start out feeling irritable and even a little upset for no reason; but as you continue to make a conscious decision to get out of the bed earlier, you will actually begin to train your body to do so. Before you know it, you will be waking up at 4 o' clock every morning! I'm just kidding. I'm not crazy! But, just think about what you could possibly accomplish if you can wake up thirty minutes earlier than you have to every day. You can start your day working toward your dreams, and have a feeling of accomplishment for the rest of the day.

You can even try making a pact with yourself to work for a certain amount of hours a week, and keep a chart of your progress. Consider refusing yourself one of your favorite snacks or recreations if you don't meet your goals for the week. Laziness is a tough habit to break, and it may take extreme measures to overcome it. You almost have to look at sleep as the enemy sometimes. Too much sleep and lying around, literally robs you of time that you could be using for dream pursuit. As I was looking through the Bible the other day, I decided to search for every time the word, "early" was used. If you've never done this before, try it. You will be surprised to see how many of God's people woke up early in the morning in order to get things done. The people of God that are mentioned in the Bible did not sleep in until noon! Even Jesus himself rose early to pray and seek God. When you are really passionate about something, and you want change to occur, you can't afford to be a lazy person. The greatest work is done early!

The truth is, everyone needs down time, but you have to put a limit on it when you are trying to make something happen. You have to make up your mind to sacrifice some of your down time in order to make progress toward the fulfillment of your dreams.

But, before I move on to the next hurdle that I want to discuss, I have to revisit that word, "passion." In order to stay motivated, passion is a necessity. Passion is defined as an *"intense, driving, or overmastering feeling or conviction."* Without that internal drive, you will find it very difficult to continue in the pursuit of your dreams when things get complicated. If you find that you're not passionate about your dream, you may be trying to do the wrong thing. Sometimes you have to analyze your dreams and determine if you are actually passionate about them. No passion, no drive. No drive, no success. So, ask yourself; *What motivates me? What moves me? What is the one thing that I could do for free for the rest of my life?*

I have always had a passion for writing. When I was in fifth grade, my English teacher wrote these words on my report card: *"One day, I will be able to say, I knew him when…"* By the time I made it to high school, my grades begin to suffer, but amazingly, I was always able to maintain a satisfactory grade in English and writing. College was no different. I flunked out of college because I spent more time partying than I did on my studies. But, when I look back at my transcripts I notice one thing; "A's" in all of my English classes.

While it is my dream to sell millions of copies of my books worldwide and become *a New York* Times bestseller, at the core of who I am, my passion for writing will never change. I will always be writing something; it doesn't matter if I sell a million books or ten.

Passion is absolutely imperative to your success. However, *misguided* passion can be an immediate distraction. *What do I mean?* Consider this; there is a young man who dreams of playing in the NFL. He loves the idea of playing in front of millions of people and getting paid for doing something that he loves. However, he begins to notice the new cars, the clothes, the big house, and the flashy jewelry, and he subconsciously changes his dream from playing in the NFL to becoming rich and possessing material things. His passion turns into wanting to become wealthy, which is a mere by-product of his initial dream; playing in the NFL. Whoops! Talk about a mistake. Now, he loses focus on the work that it takes to become an NFL player because all he can see is the money.

What the young man forgot is that the wealth was going to be there no matter what. The wealth is a result of becoming a professional football player. For this young man, his misguided passion proved to be fatal to his dream pursuit.

Whatever you do, don't lose focus on the main goal. I've heard a number of people say, "keep the main thing the main thing." So, what is *your* passion? Is your dream your passion, or are you enamored with the by-products that your dream would provide?

Your dream must be your passion, not the by-product of your dream manifestation.

Say, for instance, you want to be an actor; your passion has to be becoming the best actor you can be. Learn how to present different emotions as realistically as possible, and work on memorizing lines. Don't worry about the fame. If you are a great actor, that will come.

In my opinion, what is particularly sad about a story like the one I just mentioned is the fact that the young man obviously had that thing called *potential*. Potential is defined as something that is *"possible but as yet not actual;"* and I believe this word has derailed many a man's dreams. Someone had probably told the young man that he had potential, and the young man relaxed on his work, not realizing that potential without work is nothing. Much like faith without works is dead, so is potential.

This next hurdle can be extremely crippling to your dream pursuits. I'm talking about your *mentality*. How do you think about your dreams? Do you actually believe your dream is possible? Your mentality—your frame of mind—is of critical importance to whether or not you will be able to put yourself in position to succeed.

If you believe in God, you must believe that all things are possible. In Matthew 19:26, Jesus said, "with God all things are possible." With many dreams being immense in nature, if you don't believe those words from Jesus, it will be very hard to follow through on the pursuit of your dreams.

Lastly, another difficult hurdle to deal with as a dreamer is discouragement. When I began to think about how often I find myself discouraged, I felt like I needed to write a chapter dedicated to this subject alone. As dreamers, discouragement is just a part of the territory that you and I reside in. Hopefully the next chapter will help you to deal with discouragement properly so that it won't hinder the process of your dream pursuit.

Chapter 3

The Hurdle Called Discouragement

Discouragement is something that I know very well. It almost seems as if the more I try to encourage others in the pursuit of their dreams, the more discouraged I find myself.

One thing you have to know about discouragement is that it is simply a device of the enemy. Many times, I believe God allows the devil to see a glimpse of your future, and what the devil sees enrages him to the point that he does all that he can to keep you from fulfilling your destiny. Ahhh, destiny....we'll talk about that later.

Anyhow, when I finished the second chapter of this book, the thought came into my mind; *who do you think you are? You can't write a book. You don't even have a degree in anything.* I must say; initially, this thought was very discouraging. But, almost as if a light clicked on in my mind, I had the distinct realization that this was an attack of the enemy. I had started writing (key word; started) several books before this one, but I had never finished any. Not only that; but I had never had that kind of thought come into my mind when I was attempting to write any of the other books. It became blatantly obvious to me that God had allowed the devil to see that this time would be different. God allowed him to see the end-product, and he wanted to discourage me enough to give up on writing this book. But, instead of discouraging me, the attack actually empowered me to continue writing. God had permitted the enemy to attack my mind, but only because he knew that I had grown to a place where I could handle it.

Discouragement can come from so many different angles. It can be very discouraging to know that you have a great idea, but not have the financial stability to invest in it the way you want to. It can also be discouraging to work on dream pursuit for years without seeing any real results. As I stated earlier, I believe that being a dreamer puts you in direct conflict with the enemy. It is his desire that we see all of our problems and difficulties as too much to bear, and simply give up. When we continue to strive for something better, he has to pull out all the stops. He wants us to stay where we are instead of believing that we can achieve greater things in the future. Quite honestly, the devil doesn't want you to have a future. I believe this is why God clearly sets himself apart from the enemy in Jeremiah 29:11, and states that he will give us a "future and a hope."

When you allow yourself to dream of better days ahead, you are actually setting your hope on a brighter future. You are showing signs of faith. "Faith," "hope," and "future," are three words that the enemy despises. Therefore, it shouldn't surprise you when he aggressively pursues you with discouragement from every side.

So, how can you stay encouraged?

Well, for the answer to this question, I think we need to take a page out of David's playbook. In the book of Samuel, chapter 30, we see that David did something that we must all do from time to time; *he encouraged himself.*

Let's read;

> "And it came to pass, when David and his men were come to Ziklag on the third day, that the Amalekites had invaded the south, and Ziklag, and smitten Ziklag, and burned it with fire; And had taken the women captives, that were therein: they slew not any, either great or small, but carried them away, and went on their way. So David and his men came to the city, and, behold, it was burned with fire; and their wives, and their sons, and their daughters, were taken captives. Then David and the people that were with him lifted up their voice and wept, until they had no more power to weep. And David's two wives were taken captives, Ahinoam the Jezreelitess, and Abigail the wife of Nabal the Carmelite. And David was greatly distressed; for the people spake of stoning him, because the soul of all the people was grieved, every man for his sons and for his daughters: **but David encouraged himself in the LORD his God.**"

In these verses, David and his soldiers returned to the city of Ziglag only to find that their children and wives had been taken captive by the Amalekites. Imagine that. You have just returned to your home from a three day business trip and you find that your house has been burned to the ground, and the police tell you that your spouse and children have been kidnapped. What a phenomenal tragedy! This is exactly what David and his soldiers returned home to. This calamity proved to be more than his soldiers could deal with, and they began to blame David. They even began to speak of stoning him. But, what did David do? *"David encouraged himself in the Lord his God."* At this point, who else could David turn to? Everyone that he trusted had turned their back on him. No one in his camp was going to give him a word of encouragement. So, David took matters into his own hands; *he encouraged himself.* Can you recall the last time you spoke a word of encouragement to yourself? You don't have to stand in the middle of the mall and yell out loud so that everyone can hear; I mean, I don't want anyone to think you're crazy! But, it's ok to tell yourself, "I can do this. I'm not going to quit. My dream is not going to die. God has great plans for my life."

David knew something that many of us know, but we don't take advantage of. One of the secrets of success is to stay encouraged, which means that sometimes we have to encourage ourselves. There are times when we will almost yearn for someone to come along and encourage us; even though we can't always tell everyone what's going on (That's a chapter in itself!). In those times, you would be best advised to look to God's word for encouragement, instead of waiting for someone to miraculously come by and speak just the right words that you need to hear.

One thing that caught my attention as I pondered those words, *"David encouraged himself in the Lord his God,"* is the fact that the word, "his" was included. The Almighty, and ever-present God, had become *his* God at this particular time. Have you ever had points in your life when you didn't care who else called Him their God, you needed Him to be *your* God? This is the awesomeness of God in my opinion. He can be everywhere at the same time. He can be everyone's God at the same time. Yet, when you need Him to be yours, He can be. God is truly amazing. We all need a personal experience with God at times. Corporate worship and corporate communion is great, but there are times when I need God all to myself, and thankfully, He is always able to be there for me when I need personal time with Him. God is not a "respecter of persons," so what He does for me, He will do the same for you. It's up to you to call on Him, and reach out to Him in prayer. As a dreamer, this is essential for you! How do you expect to hold on to the faith it takes to dream if you don't feed your faith with personal time with the Lord?

It's also up to us to use the Word to fight the enemy, and encourage ourselves in difficult times. It is in our times alone with God that we learn to make the Word more personal. In order to be successful encouraging ourselves in the Word, we *must* make it personal. Not only that, but God himself has to be personal to you as well. You have to be close enough to him to know that he is indeed *your* God.

David knew that when all else failed, and all hope seemed to be lost he could always look to *his* God for encouragement and strength. Sure, you and I aren't dealing with an army of men who want to stone us to death, but we are dealing with the enemy of our dreams constantly attacking us with confusion and thoughts of doubt about our future. In order for you to stand in the face of adversity and hold on to your dreams, you must refuse to wait for others to give you the encouragement that you need. Instead, encourage yourself in the Lord *your* God.

It is absolutely imperative that we learn to lift ourselves up. It's not easy to hold on to a dream when everything around you suggests that it's pointless. You hear the enemy speaking into your mind, "It'll never happen. You might as well give up." Yet, you must hold on. You must keep fighting. Take the power of the Word in hand and leap over that hurdle called discouragement!

We've got to learn to rock to our own music. At the time that I'm writing this, my son, Michael III, is 10 months old. Whenever he becomes upset or sad about something, he sits up and starts rocking. He doesn't need any music. He just rocks to his own beat. Before long, there's a smile on his face and he is ready to tear the house up again. If only we could go back to our childhood ways sometimes. If only we could simply rock to our own music. When we learn to rock to our own music, we're no longer waiting for words of encouragement that *may* come from others. We all need encouragement from others on occasion, but if we can't encourage ourselves at times, we will find it difficult to stay motivated.

Remember, the dream that is inside of you needs to become reality; not only for your sake, but for the sake of those around you as well.

So, now that we have discussed several hurdles that stand in your way when it comes to making dream pursuit a priority, the next thing you must do, is face the music. You have to analyze yourself and pinpoint your weaknesses.

With that being said, what kind of dreamer are you?

In order to really begin to see progress toward our dreams, it is important that we identify what kind of dreamer we are and begin to deal with our own reality.

Chapter 4

What Kind of Dreamer are You?

Being a wide-awake dreamer, who wishes to actually accomplish something, requires you to be totally honest with yourself. In this chapter, I want you to make a self-assessment. I am going to discuss several kinds of dreamers that I believe exist, and somewhere in the discussion, you should be able to find yourself.

1. Wanderer

A wanderer is a dreamer who simply has a wandering mind. No focus. No direction. His "dreams" are nothing more than a collection of random thoughts. A wanderer cannot function on a high level at any of his endeavors because his mind is always wandering from one thing to the next. This person can be one of the most unproductive dreamers because I think it's actually possible to fool yourself into thinking that you accomplished something, simply because you spent time allowing your mind to wander. This, to me, is the essence of a daydreamer, but not a wide-awake dreamer. A daydreamer has no controlled thought process; his thoughts are not actually focused on his dreams. Instead, he simply allows his mind to wander just as a nomad wanders from place-to-place. A wanderer never puts anything into action; he just spends countless hours thinking about what it would be like if his dreams of having a better life magically became reality. Sadly, many people are wanderers (with an "a"), and wonderers (with an "o"). Their minds are filled with wandering thoughts and dreams, but instead of working toward them, they sit and wonder how their life would be different if their dreams came true.

You may be a Wanderer if…

- *you sit and think about your dreams, but are not planning for progress.*
- *you spend time during your workday thinking about your dream, but you don't work on it after you get off.*
- *you spend a great deal of time imagining your dreams are fulfilled, but fail to do anything to make them happen.*

---

2. Starter

A starter is a dreamer who starts the process of dream pursuit, but never actually finishes anything. What's so disappointing about being a starter is the fact that you have such zeal and fire when you first start a dream project, but as soon as the test, trials, and discouragement comes, the starter always loses his determination. As a starter, you always find yourself captivated with the next great idea without making any progress on the last great idea. Being a starter is very unproductive because there is always a level of guilt that goes along with seeing so many unfinished projects.

If you realize that this sounds like you, it's time to stop the madness. You aren't going anywhere! Being a starter is a total waste of time and effort; it's like getting in your car to go to the store, and instead of putting the car in "drive," you sit in your driveway and spin your wheels for several hours with the emergency brake on! As a starter, the joke is on you. You appear to others to be working extremely hard, but you're only spinning your wheels.

What you have to do, is decide to COMMIT. For you, your problem is your lack of commitment. When you are committed to something, you will endure the trials, headaches, and disappointment that come along with whatever you are committed to. In a marriage, for instance, there are times of adversity that are just a part of being married. However, as a husband, you have stated a vow of commitment to your marriage that you cannot renege on; no matter the difficulty. In much the same way, you must commit to your dream. Commit to see it through to the end.

You may be a Starter if...
- *you start the process of dream pursuit, but lose your zeal and leave many projects unfinished.*
- *you start the process of dream pursuit, but have not made any significant progress on any of your dream efforts.*
- *you are very excited to begin a dream project, but become discouraged when things don't seem to go your way and move on to something else.*

---

3. *Talkative*

You've met a talkative dreamer before haven't you? These are the types of people who constantly have a new idea to talk about, but in all actuality, they are doing very little if anything as it pertains to dream pursuit. A talkative dreamer just loves to talk. They will spend hours telling you about all the projects that they are working on, but if you were able to watch them during their day, you would be disappointed to see that much of what they're talking about is just that: TALK.

The biggest problem with being a talkative dreamer is the fact that you can convince yourself that you're working harder than you really are, just by talking about all the things that you are doing. It naturally feels good to talk about your progress toward the fulfillment of a dream, even if it's really not what it seems. If you find yourself talking more, and doing less, it's probably time for you to take a break from the talking and get back to reality. You may even have to submit yourself to a "hush rule," and refuse to talk about your dream for awhile. Whatever you do, don't lie to yourself. You know if you're really getting anything done or not. It doesn't benefit you in any way to talk about your progress, when in fact, there really isn't any. If you are a talkative dreamer, understand this; you may be able to fool everyone for a short time, but eventually, it will be very obvious that you spent more time talking about your dreams than you actually spent working toward them.

> *You may be a Talkative dreamer if you...*
> + *spend more time talking about your dreams than you spend actively pursuing them.*
> + *feel the need to discuss your dream pursuit even when you're really not the topic of a particular conversation.*
> + *feel pressure to compete with others when you talk about your dream pursuit.*

4. Busybody

A busybody dreamer has too many dreams to keep up with. This person is excited to start working on another dream every week. The only problem is; they are excited and motivated about so many dreams that they don't typically make any progress on any of them. Dream after dream whets their appetite for success, but their focus is so thoroughly spread out, they don't have the time to work on any of the ideas long enough to bring anything into fruition.

If you're anything like me, you've probably found yourself in a busybody state before. I have always been the type of person who thinks a lot, and most of my thinking has been about several dreams that I would like to pursue. However, in the past, I have spread myself so thin that I frequently found myself moving from one thing to the next before ever really getting a foothold on any of the projects.

While it's virtually impossible to stop yourself from being a busy-minded person, I believe it would benefit you to limit the amount of dream projects that you work on at any given time;

especially if you find that you are leaving some things undone just for the thrill of starting something new.

Lately, I have been using an *umbrella* technique to help me decide which dream projects to pursue. It's a simple concept, and it may help you as well.

First, set a main category for dream pursuit. Next, evaluate every dream project that comes to mind and consider whether it fits under the umbrella of the main dream pursuit category. If it does, pursue it. If it doesn't, put it on hold. If you use this technique you will be able to stay focused on your main dream pursuit much more easily, and avoid becoming a busybody dreamer.

> *You may be a Busybody dreamer if you…*
> + *have been working on so many dream projects that you can't concentrate on any one of them.*
> + *frequently feel overwhelmed by how many dream projects you are working on.*
> + *can't discuss in detail the dream projects that you are pursuing.*

5. Lazy

This one is really simple. A lazy dreamer is one who may have great ideas, but refuses to work. Many times, lazy dreamers have some of the most interesting and potentially lucrative ideas, but because they won't put up any effort to make things happen, they are destined to live with regret. As we talked about in the previous chapter, laziness robs you of valuable time for dream pursuit. I'll say it again; as a dreamer, you can't afford to be lazy.

You may be a Lazy dreamer if you...
- *spend time thinking about your dreams, but don't work toward fulfilling them.*
- *have off time and use it all to sleep or sit around.*
- *can remember ideas from years past that you put off, and are now living with regrets.*
- *find yourself making excuses about not having enough time to pursue your dreams.*

---

6. Progressive

Last, but certainly not least, is the progressive dreamer. The progressive dreamer will not stop working toward their dreams no matter what obstacles they may face. It doesn't matter how long it takes to see large-scale results, this person will simply not quit.

A progressive dreamer is all about progress. Webster's Online Dictionary describes "progress" in two very interesting phrases; *"positive development that is usually of the gradual kind,"* and *"motion toward something."* Go ahead, let that marinate for a few minutes. I'll wait.

As dreamers, we must decide to continue in the effort to make *motion toward* our goals. I've always heard people say, "Keep your eyes on the big picture." But, sometimes, when you dream extraordinary dreams, the big picture can be quite overwhelming. For you and I, it may suit us to keep our eyes on the small picture until the big picture appears. The progressive dreamer does just that. In their mind's eye, they see what their big picture looks like, but their attention and focus is on the small daily steps that it takes to make a dream a reality.

You are a Progressive dreamer if you...

+ *make dream pursuit a daily activity.*
+ *are content to make small steps toward your dream fulfillment.*
+ *have a mind that is dead set on making your dreams a reality, no matter how difficult it becomes.*
+ *are the kind of person who tries something, sees that it doesn't work, and instead of getting frustrated, you simply try something else.*

So, what kind of dreamer are you?

You may find that you fall into more than one category. For instance, it's possible to be a starter and a busybody at the same time. The fact is; if you can't look at your current state and say without a shadow of a doubt that you are a progressive dreamer, you are shortchanging yourself.

For some people, it's possible to fall into one of the categories that seem to be negative, but still be a progressive dreamer at the same time. For example, my little brother, Patrick, is most certainly a busybody dreamer. If you asked him, he would tell you himself. However, he happens to be the kind of person who can multi-task his dream pursuits very effectively. Thus, he tends to still get things done. Once again, the important thing is to know yourself. You know what works and what doesn't work.

Whatever you do, it's well past time to decide that you are no longer going to sit idly by and watch your dream crumble to pieces right before your eyes. You have a dream inside of you that could potentially help millions of people. It's time to take a step-by-step approach to dream pursuit, and watch your dream slowly manifest itself.

As dreamers, one thing that we have to understand is that there is no such thing as an *overnight success*. Being a progressive dreamer is really the only logical approach to dream pursuit.

Yeah, I know, we've all heard of the person who was singing their favorite song while pumping gas and the CEO of a major record company happened to be pumping gas right next to them. Bam! The next thing you know, the person is signed to a record deal and selling millions of records. Stories like this *do* happen. But for every one of these stories, there are hundreds of stories that include people who had to work for years just to get the *opportunity* to sing in front of an influential person in the industry. Then, there's the person who had to record several albums, distribute them locally, and perform at everything from birthday parties to high school talent shows, just to get someone to listen to them.

Because the overnight success stories are so extremely rare, my philosophy is this; *I cannot count on getting a "big break." I have to be a progressive dreamer and make daily movement toward my dream. Big breaks don't just happen, big breaks are made.*

I admit, as a younger man, I didn't necessarily feel that way. I used to think that you simply had to be in the right place at the right time, and good things would happen for you. As I've gotten older, I understand that dream manifestation is more about doing the work than it is about being in the right place. If you do the work, you will eventually be in the right place; that's inevitable.

I personally refuse to sit around and hope for something to happen in my life. If I want to pursue a singing career, for instance, I am going to do everything humanly possible to make it happen.

Sometimes, media; including music videos and television shows, give us the wrong impression. Because the stories about people who have seemingly gone from rags to riches in a matter of days are so impressive, these stories are drilled into our minds, and we start to think that simply waiting on a big break is a viable option. In order for us to be productive, we've got to promptly hit the delete button on that *entire* idea. Waiting on a big break is *not* a sensible option. It's not a realistic possibility. It's all about the work, time, and effort you are willing to put in.

It always boggles my mind when I see the guy, who is not overtly talented, and yet he maintains a roster spot on a professional sports team, while there are several hundred other guys who are much more talented, but they can't make a team. What is it that separates guy A from guy B? Work ethic. Some people are willing to work. Others rely solely on their talent, and fall short.

I would be amiss to say that you won't eventually need help from someone of influence, but the most important thing is to commit to the work that is necessary to succeed.

Chapter 5

Dealing with the "Meantime"

For many people, life throws so many changes at you, that oftentimes, it's just too difficult to even consider taking time to pursue dreams.

But the truth is, no matter how determined you are to see your dream become a reality, we all have to deal with the meantime on our way to dream time. I know, that was sort of corny, but you get the point. The meantime can be a very difficult time. If you're anything like me, you might find yourself sitting at your desk or taking orders over the counter while thinking to yourself, "Why am I doing this? There has got to be more to my life than where I am right now." It can be very difficult to encourage yourself to continue to work a job that seems to have nothing at all to do with where you see yourself in the future. However, as Christians, there is one verse that we must keep in mind as we deal with our meantime employment situation.

Colossians 3:23-24 says;

Michael Ford II

> "And whatsoever ye do, do it heartily, as
> to the Lord, and not unto men;
> Knowing that of the Lord ye shall receive the reward
> of the inheritance: for ye serve the Lord Christ."

The Message Bible says it like this,

> "Work from the heart for your real Master, for God,
> confident that you'll get paid in full when you come
> into your inheritance. Keep in mind always that
> the ultimate Master you're serving is Christ."

The author instructs us to work "as to the Lord." In other words, whether we're sitting at a desk bored out of our minds, loading heavy boxes into trucks on a hot and humid summer day, picking up other people's garbage, taking orders over the counter, or selling insurance, we are to do the work as if God, himself, is our boss.

Trust me; I know what it's like to have to work jobs that are totally unfulfilling. For the majority of us, it's just a part of life, especially when you have children and spouses that you have to support. But, when we do our work "as to the Lord," it helps to relieve the stress of having a job that is not particularly enjoyable.

Remember, as a dreamer, even if you only have one "9 to 5," you still have another job to do when you punch out. As a matter of fact, during your breaks on the job, if you have an opportunity to work on something that relates to your dream pursuit, do it. It only

38

makes common sense to take advantage of every free moment that you have. I remember one occasion when I took a fifteen minute break at work. After relaxing for a few minutes, I decided to turn on the computer and start working on a writing project that I had been spinning around in my mind for a few days. Unfortunately, my boss ended up walking into the office while I was typing. She let me know that I couldn't work on outside opportunities on the company computer, so I didn't get much done. But, it was definitely worth a try!

Let's face it; if you really intend to make your dreams a reality, you have to look at your dream pursuit as another job. Many of us are only working our everyday jobs just to give us enough money to take care of our responsibilities. Trust me; I understand how overwhelming this can be. However, I decided that I owe it to myself to take time to pursue my dreams despite the fact that I have to deal with the reality of working a job in order to take care of my business at home. You owe it to yourself as well. I know, I know, you may be saying, "How many times are you going to say, 'I owe it to myself'"? All I can say is...get used to it; it's just one of the philosophies that I live by. We deal with so much during the course of every day. We spend so much time helping others. Sometimes, we have to take time out to help ourselves. Why should I spend eight hours every day making someone else's dream come true, but neglect my own? I refuse.

The problem with many people is that they allow their meantime situation to drain them of their enthusiasm. They begin to lose hope and before long, complacency sets in. The worst thing a dreamer can do is to become complacent and comfortable with their present situation. Although you have to deal with the meantime, you don't have to like it, and you don't have to forget about your dreams. As you go through this present season in your life, you must have a made-up mind in order to keep the fire of your dream burning.

Albeit, with so much going on in your life, it would be easy to lose your mind!

When you feel like your mind is running to and fro, remember the words of Isaiah 26:3. It reads; "Thou wilt keep him in **perfect peace**, whose mind is stayed on thee: because he trusteth in thee."

This verse has proven to be such a blessing to me over the past few years. It informs us that if we make a conscious decision to keep our minds "stayed" on the Lord, we will experience a perfect kind of peace. You may ask, "What does it mean to keep your mind stayed on the Lord?" Well, I think it's rather simple; think about the Lord all day. Yeah, I know, this is virtually impossible. With so many things vying for your attention and so much work to do, it can seem like your mind is on everything but the Lord at times. But, once again, it's up to you to make the decision to think about the goodness of the Lord throughout the course of your day. This verse does not mean that we have to solely think about God for every minute of every day. That would be impossible. It does, however, mean that we should allow thoughts of God to dominate our mind, instead of thoughts of discontentment.

Philippians 4:8 says, "Finally, brethren, whatsoever things are true, whatsoever things are honest, whatsoever things are just, whatsoever things are pure, whatsoever things are lovely, whatsoever things are of good report; if there be any virtue, and if there be any praise, think on these things." If we allow our minds to be saturated with these kinds of thoughts, we show God that despite our current circumstances, we trust Him to make things work out for our good, and in return, we set ourselves up to experience a perfect peace. In Philippians 4:7, this same peace is described as the "peace of God that passeth all understanding." In other words, a person that keeps thoughts of God on their mind will enjoy a sense of peace that is unexplainable and beyond even your understanding. You may even find yourself asking yourself, "Why do I have such peace about this situation?" That is what you call peace that "passeth all understanding."

Yes, my friend, you can have peace even while working a job that is unrewarding or difficult. Simply remind yourself that your true boss is the Lord, and keep your mind stayed on Him.

You know, I don't know about you, but I've gotten to the place where I just refuse to give the enemy the satisfaction of seeing me sit around having a pity party about the details of my life. God has just been too good to me. Not to mention the fact that the *woe is me* mentality is unhealthy on a lot of fronts. In particular, it can cause you to sink into a rut of resentment toward God, and it paralyzes your drive to succeed. Why? Well, when you spend too much time feeling sorry for yourself, you are helpless to bring about the changes that you desire to see in your life, because you are wasting precious time sulking instead of progressing.

You have to remind yourself, daily, that you are on your way somewhere, even if it doesn't feel like it. As long as you are utilizing the time that is available to you to pursue your dream, you are still moving in the right direction. Know this; your current situation is just a detour. But, if you are committed to the struggle of dream pursuit, you know that a detour slows you down a bit, but eventually you will reach your desired destination. Not only that, but as a man of God, you should be content with whatever situation you find yourself in. In Philippians 4:11, Paul says, *"Not that I speak in respect of want: for I have learned, in whatsoever state I am, therewith to be content."* For a progressive dreamer, this word, "content" can be sort of irritating. That's because many times, we confuse this word to mean complacency, when that's not the case at all. To be content in your present circumstances is to be satisfied with the Lord and the course that he is allowing your life to take. The *content* that Paul is speaking of is more of an *intent* to be thankful in every situation, than it is a decision to stay in the place that he was.

Even as you press toward the fulfillment of your dreams, you should allow yourself to be thankful at all times. When Paul penned those words, he was sitting inside of a dirty jail cell, imprisoned for following the leading of the Lord; an unfair situation for a man of God if you ask me. However, what we have to realize is that life is not always fair. But, it's always better to be in the will of God than outside of it. I am determined, like Paul, to be thankful no matter what. As I stated before, God has been too good to me. I have a house to live in, clothes on my back, and food in my refrigerator. I won't sit around and complain simply because I have to work a job that I don't like or deal with people that don't appreciate what I have to offer. It would be in your best interest to take on the attitude of thankfulness in your meantime season.

The same man that said he had learned to be content in any situation also said that he was pressing *"toward the mark for the prize of the high calling of God in Christ Jesus."* Paul was not much different than you and I. Undoubtedly, he had dreams and goals than he hoped to attain. So, he was willing to go through whatever obstacles were placed in his way in order to take hold of the prize that he sought.

In your meantime season, press toward seeing the realization of your dreams, but be satisfied with the Lord, intent to be thankful, and God will help you through your struggles.

You have to realize that God is trying to teach you something about yourself in your present situation. He is preparing you for a great future, but you have to be patient with the process and patient with the Lord. At one time in my life, my pastor, Reverend Hurley Coleman Jr., noticed frustration in my demeanor as I struggled with the fact that I was in place that looked nothing like what my dreams suggested to me.

"Mike, what's going on?" He asked.

"Pastor, I just don't understand what's going on with my job. It just seems like I'm not going anywhere. This just isn't how I envisioned my life, man."

"You've got to trust God, man." He replied.

"I'm trying to," I said, "but I know there's got to be something more for me to be doing with my life."

"Learn all you can where you are Mike." Pastor informed.

"What do you mean?"

"The job that you're working right now does not have to be the end for you, but God is teaching you some things right where you are. Learn all you can."

"Ok." I said.

Many times, we look so far ahead that we don't allow ourselves to see the benefit of our present moments. We spend so much time yearning for a better tomorrow that we fail to learn what God is trying to teach us today. In whatever situation you find yourself in right now, there is always something that you can learn; right where you are.

As I look back at that time in my life, I realize that the thing I was most discouraged about is the fact that my job seemed to be such a menial, irrelevant position. The menial nature of the jobs that many of us find ourselves having to work tends to make us feel as though our position in life is insignificant. We can even start to believe that we are outside of the will of God. This is not always the case. In your meantime situation, God is preparing you for something greater; and the truth is, he expects you to produce right where you are. In Matthew 25, there is a story of a wealthy landowner who placed his goods in the care of his servants while he went on a long trip. To one servant he gave five talents (a measurement of money), to another servant, he gave two talents, and to yet another, he gave one talent. Upon the owner's return from his trip, he found that the one who had been given five talents had gained five additional talents, the one who had been given two talents had gained two more, and the servant who had been entrusted with one talent had not gained any additional talents. The owner was pleased with the two servants who had increased their lot, but he was thoroughly upset with the servant who had simply buried his talent in the ground and returned it to him without profit.

Of course Jesus used this parable to illustrate the fact that as men of God, we are to use our God-given abilities to impact the kingdom of God and win souls to salvation. But, I want to look at this story from another angle. From the onset of the story, it may seem as if the owner was being unfair. He gave five talents to one servant, two to another, and only one to the last servant. Why? Well, if you read Matthew 25:15, you see that the owner distributed the goods according to their *"several ability."* The owner had been around the men long enough to know their capabilities. Therefore, he gave them what he knew they had the *potential* to succeed with, based on their own level of skill and knowledge. In the same way, God knows us better than we know ourselves. He places talents and abilities in our hands that are tailor-made to fit who he made us to be, and even orchestrates the circumstances of our lives to lead us to a particular place.

It doesn't matter if you feel you have been given two talents or twenty, God expects you to produce in your present situation. After receiving the news that the two servants had turned his money into a profit, the owner expressed his pleasure by telling them, *"Well done, good and faithful servant; thou hast been faithful over a few things, I will make thee ruler over many things."*

Those servants received a promotion! When it becomes apparent to God that you are willing to put forth the effort to please Him in every situation, he will make you a ruler over many things as well. Consider this: If you can't be trusted to pay your tithes making $500 a week, why would God trust you with $10,000 a week? Not only that, but if you cannot be faithful with the job that you currently have, why would God allow you to achieve your dream position? If you neglect to acknowledge God in your present situation, why would he advance you to the next level? Remember, you are a man of God, so you can't expect things to happen for you in the same way that they happen for men of the world.

Every job has significance in the life of a man of God. Every task is credible. You must decide to get the most out of your current situation. To waste time sulking is pointless.

As you deal with your meantime season, understand this; God is preparing you for something great. He has a great plan for your life, and many times, your dreams are a direct reflection of the plan of God for your life.

However, it is possible that we would have a dream that doesn't line up with the will of God. Once again, that's why, as children of God, we have to be patient. He knows what's best for us. It may be that He is taking you on a detour just to slow you down long enough to show you that your dream needs to be refined in order to line up with His will for your life. And, trust me; God's will is the best thing for you.

If you find that your dream does not line up with God's will for your life, it would be better for you to alter your dream to fit His will than to try to convince yourself that your dream is acceptable anyhow.

As you go through your meantime, it helps to remember that there are others who are going through the same thing that you are going through. You are not alone. You have to understand that your current situation is just a part of the process.

Stop having a pity party! Stop feeling sorry for yourself! These things are not productive. Every great person had to deal with a meantime situation at one time or another. 1 Corinthians 10:13 says, "There hath no temptation taken you but such as is **common** to man: but God is faithful, who will not suffer you to be tempted above that ye are able; but will with the temptation also make a way to escape, that ye may be able to bear it." This verse is generally used to encourage us as we go through the daily struggle of trying to please God with our lives, but I subscribe to the fact that it can encourage you as a dreamer as well. It reminds us that the temptations and struggles that we face are not new. They have been around for ages. People have been dealing with these same struggles since the beginning of time. The devil would love to make you feel as if you are alone in your struggles. <u>But, you are not alone.</u> The problems that you are facing are common issues for all mankind, and they do not make you an outsider. My friend, you are not an anomaly.

Let's take a look at a couple of verses to get a better understanding:

<u>1 Peter 5:8</u>

"Be sober, be vigilant; because your adversary the devil, as a roaring lion, walketh about, seeking whom he may devour."

<u>John 10:10</u>

*"The thief cometh not, but for to **steal**, and to **kill**, and to **destroy**: I am come that they might have life, and that they might have it more abundantly."*

Take your time and think about those two verses, and you will see clearly why the devil wants you to feel like you're alone. If he can cause you to believe that you are going through a struggle that sets you apart from others, he's got you right where he wants you. For most of us, when we're going through something that seems to be odd, or makes us look bad, we won't discuss these things with anyone. We will keep them bottled up inside for fear of appearing to be weak or inadequate. That's when we make trouble for ourselves. We all need to be able to talk to others in order to understand the dynamics of our own life, but if we feel like our situation is unique, we won't even bother. Therefore, we end up in a very lonely situation, and lonely people are extremely vulnerable to attacks from the enemy. If you've ever watched one of those animal programs on TV, you may have seen how lions hunt for their prey. The Bible states that the devil is as a "roaring lion…seeking who he may devour."

Lions never fight fair. They purposefully and very strategically target the weakest and loneliest deer or gazelle in the bunch to pursue. As soon as they spot the easiest target, they pounce. This is the very nature of Satan. He pursues you the hardest when you are at your weakest point; when you feel alone. His desire is to completely destroy you; mind, body, and soul.

However, although we know the enemy is hard on our heels, we can be encouraged in the fact that we know God comes into our midst to lead us into an abundant life. As I stated a few paragraphs ago, your meantime situation is just a part of the process. Therefore, pick your head up and go forward, knowing that the Lord is on your side.

The Bible declares in Romans 8:31, "What shall we then say to (all) these things? If God be for us, who can be against us?"

With the Lord on our side, we can stand under the pressures of life. However, over the years, I've learned that there's one enemy that is very tough to deal with. Who am I talking about? Read on to find out.

Chapter 6

Your Biggest Opponent

In order to really see the fulfillment of your dreams, you have to realize that your biggest opponent is not the guy next door, or the girl in your classroom who seems to know all of the answers. Instead, your most intense competitor, and the one who has the most power to sabotage your efforts is.....you.

So many people put extra pressure on themselves, because they insist on paying too much attention to others rather than focusing on themselves. You can't spend your time watching others and expect to make something happen in your own life. When it comes to dream fulfillment, coveting the success of others will get you nowhere. It's not about anyone else. It's about you and what you are willing to do to make your own dreams come true.

You may have a dream to become a doctor. But, you're forty years old and someone else that you know became a doctor at twenty-eight. So what!!?? But, you barely graduated from high school. Who cares!!?? You don't have to compete with anyone. It could be that that person didn't have to face the obstacles that you had to face in your life. Or, it could be that they were more dedicated in their youth than you were. Whatever the case may be, your time is now. It's time for you to make a decision about your dream. Do you want it or not? How bad do you want it?

I know I've used that word, "decision" more times than the word, "thee" was used in the Bible; but the truth is, every great individual accomplishment begins with a decision. Not the decisions of others, but the decision of the individual. You must understand; no matter whom the President is, or how bad the economy is, or who doesn't like your ideas, your decisions have the greatest impact on your future. No one can affect your future like you can. So, don't give anyone else that power.

I'll say it again; *you're biggest competitor is yourself.*

Have you ever come in contact with someone who is so competitive with others, that it stifles their growth?

Then, there are those who pay so much attention to others' accomplishments, that it becomes painfully obvious that they are jealous. As a wide-awake dreamer, you can't afford to be covetous of the success of others. You've got your own dreams to be concerned about. Why squander away precious time trying to keep up with someone else?

The fulfillment of your dream is all about you; the sacrifices you are willing to make, the time you are willing to spend, the work you are willing to put in.

You've got to remember; as you make the daily decision (and it is a daily decision) to pursue your dreams; *every little bit counts.*

If you've ever watched a workout program, then you know that many times the leader of the workouts will show viewers different ways to modify the exercises to fit their personal level of fitness and ability. But, it is always stressed that although you may not be able to keep up with the people who are on the DVD, as long as you don't quit, you will see results. This speaks to the topic of this chapter; *you are your biggest competition.*

So many people start out with the best intentions, but allow themselves to become increasingly more frustrated with each workout because they realize that they can't keep up with the individuals on the video. But, guess what? YOU DON'T HAVE TO! If a certain workout DVD is entitled Y90X (wink, wink), and you are supposed to have a dramatically different body after 90 days, it's still ok if it takes you 180 days to see the same results. You don't have to compete with anyone. Just don't quit! Quitting is really the only way to ensure that you will not succeed. Make up your mind to keep trudging along.

You've got to have a *tortoise mentality* as it concerns your dream. You remember the story of the tortoise and the hare don't you? The hare in the story was a natural runner. His entire body was formed in a way that is conducive to running. The muscles in his legs are fashioned for making huge strides and moving around quickly. The tortoise's body on the other hand, is made more for protection than participating in any physical activity. Not only are his legs short, but they are also very thick, which make it virtually impossible for him to move at a rapid pace. But, the tortoise was determined to finish the race. He knew his own weaknesses, and I'm sure he understood that he had a distinct disadvantage in comparison to the hare. He was very aware that he would have to work extremely hard just to finish the race; let alone to beat the hare.

Many of you are7 living with disadvantages: broken homes, unemployment, and disabilities, but as a dreamer, you must be determined to hold on to your dreams despite the fact that you have been dealt a bad hand. Over the course of history, the stories of individuals who have overcome the odds to fulfill their dreams are countless. In no way do I mean to diminish the fact that certain disadvantages are very difficult to deal with, but, if you intend to see your dreams come true, there has to be a point when you tell yourself, "*There are no excuses.*"

Just because no one else in your family has ever graduated from college does not mean that you won't. *There are no excuses.* You may have made some mistakes as a youth and now you have a criminal record, but if you are willing to put in the extra work, your dreams are still not out of reach. *There are no excuses.* Sure, you grew up in a single parent home, and your father was nowhere to be found, but this does not have to put a halt to your dream pursuit. *There are no excuses.*

Growing up in the rigid city of Saginaw, MI, I have witnessed many things. The city is plagued with violence, poverty, and single parent homes. In Saginaw, and cities like it, it would be easy to concede to a life of mediocrity. As a matter of fact, for many people who live in such cities, the thought of pursuing their dreams is a ridiculous thought. In my city, we are told by the vast majority of society that we might as well find a job (no matter if you like the job or not), settle in for thirty-five years, and hope that you can save enough money to be financially stable when you retire.

Retire? Are you serious? Thirty years from now, it's not even a guarantee there will be any such thing as retirement. I'm all about breaking out of the status quos. To be totally honest, status quos are offensive to me. One of the quickest ways to irritate me is to try to convince me that I have to fit into a pre-constructed box or that things will always be the way they are. No! I *do* have a say in how my life turns out. I don't have to just sit back and let life beat me up.

However, for many of us, the status quo has gone from being the "condition or state of affairs that currently exist," as defined by *Encarta* dictionary, to being the only thing we can see in our future as well. If the only thing you can see for your future is more of the same, maybe it's time for you to evaluate your surroundings. Who are you talking to? Who are you sharing your dreams with? Where do you spend your time? What are you reading? What are you watching on TV? If you're spending more time watching the news than you are reading the Word of God, there's no wonder why you can't imagine a future that's better than where you are now. The news is full of despair! I will dig a little deeper into the idea of evaluating your surroundings in the next chapter.

But, over the years, I have developed the attitude that says, *if anyone can make it out of this city and become successful, I can.* This is the kind of stance that all of us must take. Despite the outward circumstances that we find ourselves in, the main factor in making your dreams a reality always lies inside of you.

I want you to do me a favor.

Grab a blank sheet of paper. Jot down every excuse that you could possibly have for not taking time to pursue your dreams.

Your list may look something like this:

1. *I lost my job.*
2. *I don't have the experience.*

and….

3. *I'm too old.*

Take a good look at your list of excuses. Now, take your list of excuses, ball it up, and throw it in the trash. Starting today, those excuses will no longer hinder you. You have just made a powerful, outward statement to yourself, your biggest opponent. The excuses that once held you captive are now a thing of the past. Those excuses will no longer paralyze your dream pursuit; they have been destroyed and thrown away. This is a new day!

The hare in the story possessed several advantages, but he was not willing to work to his full potential. He was content just doing enough to get by. As a dreamer, this is a tragic mistake. If you are not willing to push yourself beyond your preconceived limits, seeing your dreams become reality will prove to be impossible. Neither advantages nor natural talent or ability will cover a lack of diligence and effort. Although you may reach short-term success depending solely on your natural abilities, sustained success will be out of reach. Even those who are naturally gifted have to be willing to put in the work.

I remember as a youngster, I was very intelligent. During my elementary and middle school years, I made good grades based solely on my natural intellect. Unfortunately, when I got into high school and college, natural intellect was not enough. I started getting terrible grades on my homework assignments, and testing proved to be extremely complicated. It became painfully obvious that I had to learn how to study and work hard in order to be successful in school. Trust me, it was a difficult lesson, but one that I'm glad I had the opportunity to learn.

So many people, much like the rabbit, have all the potential in the world, but their poor work ethic leads them to unfulfilled dreams and resigns them to a life of regret. As I mentioned in chapter four, as a sports fan, it always baffles me when I scan the landscape of professional sports; from Major League Baseball to the NFL, and see so many so-called "scrubs" that are getting paid millions of dollars from pro teams even though it is fairly obvious that they don't possess the inherent talent of their superstar counterparts. These *scrubs* knew that what they lacked in natural talent could be made up by simply outworking others. It all comes down to your work ethic, your internal drive to succeed, and your belief in yourself. You must understand; your dream may seem impossible to some, but the only person who absolutely *has* to believe that it is indeed possible, is you.

Although someone may have better credentials, more degrees, a deeper bank account, or a more structured family makeup, the decision to reach the finish line still lies in your hands.

To be quite honest, I don't think the problem for many of us lies in what we don't have, instead, it lies in the fact that we simply aren't committed to ourselves the way we are committed to others. We don't value our word to ourselves the way we value our word to others. *What do I mean?* Well, consider this; when was the last time you gave someone your word and then failed to do what you said you were going to do? If you're anything like me, you value your word to such a degree that you would rather say nothing at all than to say you will do something but fail to follow through. So, why do we so often fail to commit to our word when it comes to ourselves? We tell ourselves, *I'm going to enroll in school next semester,* and before we know it, the next semester is here, and we're not enrolled. We go an entire year without calling in sick or being late for work, but we continually put off any efforts to pursue our own dreams. In essence, we take days off from ourselves all the time!

I believe it is essential for us to begin to treat ourselves with the same respect that we treat others with. Keeping your word should be just as important as it relates to you and your dream as it is when you speak it to someone else. Stop selling yourself short. Stop letting yourself down.

I have had conversations with numerous people who fail to give their dreams a place of priority in their lives, and many of these people have to find something to blame for their lack of diligence. Many times, I've found that it's easy for them to simply say, "Well, I didn't have the opportunities that others had in life." Forget that! Hebrews 12:1 reminds us to "run the race that is set before us." We all have our own race to run, and if we are determined to win, we can most certainly do so.

If you haven't noticed, I am a huge sports fan, so sports analogies just seem to come natural for me. Here's another one: at the beginning of every college football season, several facets of the media put out preseason polls; ranking the top twenty-five teams in the nation. The rankings are based on the previous season, and the success that is anticipated for the upcoming season. The goal for every team is to be one of the top two teams at the end of the season so that they can play for the national championship. What's significant about this scenario is that it doesn't matter if one of the teams starts the season outside of the top two or completely unranked, they still have the opportunity to advance into the top twenty-five and even into the top two.

You have to remember, it's not about the starting position; it's about where you end up.

Take the limits off of God, and take the limits off of yourself. No one but you can put your dreams in a box; neither can anyone set the ceiling of what you can achieve unless you give them that power. Whatever you do, understand the power that you possess. You can either be your own best ally or your worst adversary in the process of pursuing your dreams.

Chapter 7

Evaluate Your Surroundings

As I stated in chapter six, for many of us, the status quo has gone from being the "condition or state of affairs that currently exist," as defined by *Encarta* dictionary, to being the only thing we can see in our future as well. If you find that you have a hard time holding on to your dreams, it's time for you to evaluate your surroundings.

In this chapter, I want you to consider a couple of questions. Part of your surroundings is what you allow to enter your mind.

With that being said, *what ideas and influences are you allowing entrance into your mind via the media that you expose yourself to?*

If you submit yourself to watching the news on a daily basis, but neglect the Word of God, it should be no wonder that you find yourself discouraged and weary all too often. The news is full of despair! You will end up a nervous wreck if you spend too much time watching that stuff!

Actually, one morning a few months ago, I turned on the news to watch it as I got ready for work. After listening for a few minutes and being irritated by how much negativity was being spewed out of the mouths of the reporters, I decided to grab a sheet of paper and write down every negative word that I heard. Over the next five minutes, I was able to jot down a list of over twenty words, including; "foreclosure," "depressing," and "disaster," just to name a few. Twenty negative words in five minutes! And, that's the way you want to start your day?

Instead of picking up your Bible for five minutes and receiving a word of encouragement and peace to begin your day, you listen to the news of the world and dress yourself in a garment of heaviness. No wonder you walk into your job with your head held down, and struggle to put a smile of your face. I encourage you to break up the monotony today!

You may have gotten to the point where a cup of coffee and the morning news is a regular routine for you. If you continually expose yourself to such hopelessness, you will find that staying motivated to pursue your dreams will be extremely difficult. Think about this; if you have a regular morning routine that does not include God, the devil has no reason not to attack your mind very early in the day. You have to put yourself in position to have a great day by safeguarding your mind early. David said it best in Psalms 63:1, "*O God, thou art my God; **early will I seek thee***: *my soul thirsteth for thee, my flesh longeth for thee in a dry and thirsty land, where no water is.*"

The societies that we live in can seem like *dry and thirsty lands*. It's easy to feel as if there is no possibility for advancement, no chance for our dreams to be fulfilled. This is why we must seek our Father in the early hours of the day.

As a dreamer, you are already working against the grain. As I stated earlier, our society doesn't exactly make it easy for people who have big aspirations for the future. So, to add to the already difficult circumstances by filling your mind with negativity is making your dream pursuit unnecessarily complicated.

Another element of your surroundings is your friends. *Who are you sharing your time with?*

Who you allow to occupy your time and energy is a huge factor in the quality of your life in general, and your ability to successfully chase your dreams. When it comes to relationships, they can have a positive impact on your pursuits or completely throw you off pace. As a dreamer, I find it very irritating to spend time with people who are negative. Negative people give off negative vibes, engage in negative conversation, and seemingly live in a negative place. These are the people who will get a promotion on their job and instead of being thankful, they find something depressing about their new position to talk about. Not only that, but if you have something positive going on in your life, they will gladly help you find something depressing in your *own* situation to talk about. Negative people just bug me!

I know, there is no way to rid your life of *all* negative people (besides, some of them are family!), but, if you want to make your dreams happen, you've got to be careful who you spend your time with. Unless you are careful, you can allow negative people to vex your spirit to such a degree, that you could actually begin to feel as if your dreams are no longer possible. As a dreamer, you've got to be the type of person who picks your friends instead of letting your friends pick you. I'm not at all suggesting that you be an arrogant person, but you can't simply allow anyone to befriend you. When it becomes apparent to you that a certain person is not helping you to achieve your dreams, it would be wise to make some changes.

As my relationship with the Lord began to develop, it became apparent to me that I needed to make some changes in the way I rationed out my time with my friends.

As much as I enjoyed spending time with them, I realized that we were going in opposite directions. I knew that if I wanted to have what God has for me, I had to be willing to show Him that I would not even allow my friends to get in the way. I made up my mind that I had to spend less time with them. We had spent numerous late nights out over the years, chasing women and getting into all sorts of sinful behavior. But, for me to prosper in the ways of the Lord, I knew I would have to sacrifice some of the time that I spent with my friends.

When I look back on that time in my life, I realize that I have some really special guys in my life. My friends never pressured me to come back to my old lifestyle. It's a blessing to be able to say that, for the most part, they all supported me one hundred percent. But, as I felt the Lord move in my life, I know that had they decided not to support me, I would have been able to let them go their way. Thank God I didn't have to completely lose them as friends. Now, several of them have a relationship with the Lord themselves. God is awesome! So guys, if you're reading this, I'm not classifying you all as negative people!

As I alluded to earlier, one of the biggest problems with negative people is that they love to engage in negative conversation; and for you the dreamer, this is completely unconstructive. When you allow yourself to indulge in negatively-charged conversation, you take the risk of defeating yourself and killing your dreams.

Let's take a look at Proverbs 18:21. It says:

"Death and life are in the power of the tongue: and they that love it shall eat the fruit thereof."

Think about that. Your tongue has power; it has the power of life and death. You can spend your time involved in negative conversations and literally speak death over your dreams; or, you can speak words of faith and infuse your dreams with life. It's really your choice.

My mom is one of the most positive and encouraging people I know. After having a conversation with her, I feel as if anything is possible. If you had a dream to reach for the moon, my mom is the type of person that will make you feel as if you may actually be able to touch it one day. I think it is vitally important to associate with people who help you to believe that all things really are possible as the Word of God says.

Speaking of my mom, I can't move on without sharing something with you. When I was about seventeen years old, I came up with a not-so-brilliant plan to get some extra money; I would steal my mom's debit card, go to the ATM, and withdraw as much money as I could. My plan probably worked three or four times. I took out $200 every time, so I think I ended up stealing roughly $800 from my own parents! Yes, I'm ashamed to admit it, but it's the truth.

Needless to say, I was aghast when I overheard my mom and dad having a conversation one night about money being mysteriously taken out of their account. After a couple of days, the bank called back and said that they had video of the perpetrator. What was I to do? I decided to come clean because it occurred to me that I would rather tell my mom myself than have her go to the bank and witness her son stealing from her on camera. Listening to my mom's lecture and seeing the pure frustration and disappointment in her eyes was one of the worst feelings I have ever had to deal with.

Yet, through my mistake, my parents taught me a lot about forgiveness. I was at an age where they could have kicked me out of the house, but they didn't. They would have had every right to press charges against me as well, but they didn't. As a matter of fact, it wasn't long before my mom was giving me her ATM password again, and sending me to the bank to get money for her. To this day, she probably still doesn't know how much it meant to me to be given another chance. Her compassion allowed me to move forward unto becoming a man of God.

The problem with many people is that they insist on trying to keep you locked into your past. Whether it's your past failures or past mistakes, some people are intent on holding you hostage in your history. As you press toward the fulfillment of your dreams, it's important that you let those who are around you know that you will not be bound to your past, and if they refuse to allow you to move on, they cannot continue to be a part of your life.

For me, negative conversation has never been something that I enjoy. I don't like gossip, and I'm not interested in a pity party dialogue. Everyone has had difficult times in life, but continuing to dwell on those memories and discuss them is neither productive nor beneficial to your dream pursuit.

When you're on the phone with someone and the conversation starts to head down a path to negativity you need to just stop them in their tracks and say, *"I don't want to hear that."* That's simple enough right? If you don't put your foot down and set limits, people will dump more trash on you than a sanitation worker picks up in an entire day. I don't know about you, but I refuse to be a *messmate*. *What is a messmate?* According to Webster's dictionary, a messmate is *"a person with whom one regularly takes mess."* Now, this word is generally used to refer to individuals on a ship who frequently share meals together. So, I'm obviously using it out of context. But, you show me a preacher who doesn't use words out of context, and I'll show you one boring preacher! Bottom line is this; I refuse to take on anyone's trash! Gossip, despair, hopelessness, pity parties, and faithless talk is not for me!

As wide-awake dreamers, we have to use the power of our tongue wisely. Proverbs 18:21 says that we will *"eat the fruit"* of our own tongue. If I spend my days speaking of my past failures and discussing the odds that are stacked against me, I am burying my faith under a sheet of unbelief, and the fruit that I will eat is failure in my dream pursuits. Once again it comes back to decisions. Realize the power that lies in your tongue and make the decision to take it very seriously. You can talk yourself out of your dreams, or speak your dreams into reality. What's your choice?

The old adage says, "Birds of a feather flock together." Sure, it's a cliché, but it's also very true. You absolutely *must* pay attention to who you are spending your time with. I've always believed that you are either going to cause people to conform to your way of life and your way of thinking or you are going to conform to their lifestyle and their way of thinking. There really is no gray area. Therefore, in many cases, it would be easier to just eliminate the temptation to think, talk, and act negatively. It may sound harsh, but until some of your friends decide that they no longer want to dwell in negativity, it may be time to eliminate them from your circle. It's just not worth the hassle to hang on to people who are dragging you down.

Another reason why you can't afford to surround yourself with negative people is because you really can't afford to share your dreams with everyone.

Joseph, the most famous dreamer in the Bible, found out the hard way that he couldn't share his dreams with everyone. Genesis 37:5 says, *"And Joseph dreamed a dream, and he told it his brethren: and they hated him yet the more."* Listen dreamer: you have got to understand this one thing; there are people in your life right now, who will smile in your face, share a cup of tea with you, go out for dinner and a movie, but still don't really care for you! And when they hear of your big dreams, don't be too surprised when they can no longer hold back their hate. It's a sad truth, but not everyone wants to see you succeed. So, be careful who you share your dreams with!

I have noticed in my life that there are so many bitter people in this world. Everyone has an opportunity to pursue change in their lives, but many people would rather make excuses for not trying and then discourage you from pursuing *your* dreams. This is why dreamers have to guard their dreams. Many people will pursue a relationship with you just so they can be nosey, figure out your plans, and ultimately cause you to fail. Again I say, be careful who you share your dreams with; this is of critical importance to your success.

When it comes to sharing your dreams, there's another point that I want to make: Although you can't talk to *everyone* about your dreams, you can't be afraid to talk about them in general. If you are afraid to talk about your dreams, you really can't expect them to come to pass. The power of life in your tongue needs to be expressed not suppressed. I have no problem at all telling people that I dream of becoming a *New York Times* bestseller. As a matter of fact, a couple of years ago I started signing my name as, "Michael Ford $" instead of "Michael Ford II." Why? Because I know that I will be wealthy someday, and I want to have an interesting story for *Ebony* magazine when they interview me in the near future.

I can hear it now:

"So, why do you sign your name with a money sign?" They'll ask.

"Well, it was just my way of making a personal declaration of wealth that I saw in my future."

That sounds pretty good doesn't it?

Talk proudly and boldly about your dreams. If you're not confident in your dreams, you can't expect anyone else to be confident in them either. You can't share your dreams with everyone, but it may help *someone* to hear you speak of the things that you hope to accomplish in life. If you make the effort to be selective about the kind of people you allow to occupy your time and energy, you won't have to worry so much about who you are sharing your dreams with anyhow.

I say again, check your surroundings.

While it is true that you have the power within you to overcome difficult circumstances and surroundings; to expose yourself to unnecessary negativity is an obstruction to your progress that you should plan to avoid if at all possible.

Chapter 8

Godly Success

Many times, people place pressure on themselves to succeed. The problem with this pressure is that often it is simply unnecessary and unproductive. I have noticed in my own life that I tend to place this kind of pressure on myself because I fail to recognize the successes that have already taken place in my life, and I discredit godly success.

Seven years ago, when I was twenty-three years old, I took a piece of paper and wrote these words on it, *"I will be a millionaire by the time I'm thirty."* Needless to say, I am now thirty years old, and I am not a millionaire! Disappointing? Absolutely. But, although I haven't acquired millions of dollars over the course of the last seven years, one could argue, that in the eyes of God, I am yet a success.

On December 17th, 2004...Oops...I mean December 18th .....(Smile)....I married the most amazing woman I have ever met. My wife, La'Shon, was surely sent from heaven directly to me. Not long after we said, *"I do,"* we welcomed a beautiful baby girl into the world. My daughter, Madison, was born on January 17th, 2006.

Our new family settled into a home that the Lord blessed us to purchase right in the middle of one of the worst economic recessions that the United States has ever seen. My wife received promotion after promotion on her job, and I was hired off the street and given a position driving for one of the major delivery companies in the world.

My wife and I became increasingly involved in our church, and we made a concentrated effort to teach our daughter the ways of the Lord, and set an example for her in words and in deeds.

Before long, I felt a call to ministry. I can remember the first time I felt like God was calling me to preach. Fear fell over me almost immediately. I felt great apprehension about the call, because I know that preaching is an enormous responsibility. I prayed, *Lord, I feel as if you're calling me to preach your Word. Please don't allow me to accept this calling if you know I'm just going to fall into sin and turn away from you.*

He didn't take his call back, so I said, "Yes," and began a journey of ministry and a pursuit to please God with my life.

Before I gave my life to Christ, I had dreams of becoming the next great R&B singing sensation. I recorded a professional demo, took several photographs and put together a packet to send to the major record companies. Unfortunately, none of the major companies took the bait. I started to feel like my dream could never happen. But, before I fell into an all-out depression, my then-girlfriend and I had an argument that changed the course of my life.

My wife and I met in a club. I'm not sure if she was drunk at the time, but I surely was. One of her good friends introduced her to me. We started talking on the phone on a regular basis, and although neither one of us were looking for anything serious, eventually, a real friendship developed, and we realized that we wanted to be in a relationship.

The argument that I spoke of previously, happened early one Sunday morning. My wife, who was my girlfriend at the time, had started to attend church on a regular basis and rekindled a relationship with the Lord that was instilled in her as a young girl. I, on the other hand, had maintained my relationship with drinking and partying every week.

She called me on that morning.

"Hey, what are you doing?" She asked.

"I'm sleep...its 8:45." I replied. I had stayed out almost all night partying. I had probably only been in the bed for about four hours at that time.

"Well, do you want to go to church with me this morning?"

I had a feeling she was going to ask me that question, because she had been asking me for weeks to come and visit her church. But, I was hung-over and extremely exhausted. There was no way I was going to *anybody's* church that morning.

"Naw, not today. I'm tired. Pray for me though."

She smacked her lips in complete disgust and said, "No, you pray for *yourself*!"

Click.

She had never hung the phone up in my face. I was surprised, but I was also thoroughly irritated.

I sat up in my bed and called her back immediately.

"Yeah, I *will* pray for myself! See you at church!"

I jumped out of bed, got dressed, and beat her to the church. I was sitting there with a smug look on my face when she walked in the door, but all she did was laugh at me.

When I look back on that morning, all I can do is laugh at me, *too*. I went to the service that day with a spiteful attitude. But, little did I know, I was right where God (and my girlfriend) wanted me in the first place. Not long after that day, I surrendered my life to Jesus.

I began to strive to live a life that would please God. My girlfriend and I started attending church together every week and throughout the week as well, and we made a conscious effort to satisfy God with our relationship. Before long, God allowed me to see a glimpse of the gift that I had in my midst. Although I hadn't spent much time thinking about marriage, my girlfriend began to take on a different appeal for me. She no longer looked like a girlfriend. I started to see her as my wife. I felt the Lord speak into my heart and say, "She's the one." I proposed to her at a concert that we were singing in together; she said, "Yes," and the rest is history.

As you can see, my life took a drastic turn for the better when I accepted Jesus Christ as my Savior. In many respects, when I step back and look at what God has done in my life, I realize that although I haven't attained some of the things that I wanted to attain, my life is already a success in the eyes of God---God is the number one priority in my life, I love my wife and I am trying to treat her in a way that makes her feel respected and appreciated, I am raising my children to love God, and I work every day to provide for my family. In God's eyes, these things are the epitome of success.

As you strive to reach the heights of dream success, take time to appreciate where you are in life right now. If you are a man who tries to live a life that pleases God, loves and supports your wife, maintains an occupation, and is taking time to be a father, you are a success right now in the eyes of God. Don't allow the enemy to make you feel like a failure. Remember, the devil is a liar, and there is no truth in him.

Chapter 9

Destiny Awaits

With all of this talk about dreams, I felt it would be an oversight for me not to mention *destiny*. As my relationship with the Lord has matured over the last few years, I have learned that *dreams* and *destiny* are two very distinct things, but they can actually work hand-in-hand. Dreams are generally derived from our own thoughts and our own desires for our lives, and they are limited because of that fact. Destiny, on the other hand, is originated in the mind of God; even before we are born into this world; it is defined as "someone's preordained future." Read the words of Ephesians 1:11: "In whom also we have obtained an inheritance, being **predestinated** according to the purpose of him who worketh all things after the counsel of his own will."

In Jeremiah 1:5 (NIV), we see destiny revealed from the heart of God: *"Before I formed you in the womb I knew you, before you were born I set you apart; I appointed you as a prophet to the nations."* Isn't that something? Even before Jeremiah came forth out of his mother's womb, God already had an outstanding plan for his life; he was to be "a prophet to the nations." Herein lies Jeremiah's destiny. But, in order for him to reach the great heights that God had planned for him, he had to surrender his life to God. As I mentioned earlier, God is not a "respecter of persons" so what he did for Jeremiah, he has also done for us. In God's infinite wisdom, he counsels within himself, and constructs destinies for us all. Destiny cannot be revealed by any other means but by a relationship with the Creator through a surrendered life.

So many people are walking around everyday confused and not having any idea what their purpose is, but they neglect the One who created them. How can anyone expect to know what they are supposed to be doing with their life without spending any time asking their Creator? If indeed you believe that God created you, you must believe that He created you for a specific reason. So, why not ask Him? It's absurd to walk through life blindfolded and wandering from place to place with no direction. God is ready and willing to speak to you concerning your destiny.

Dreams and destiny, while completely different things, can work together as long as you are willing to have your dreams refined as I mentioned in an earlier chapter. You have to be willing to submit your dreams to God in order to have destiny. According to Jeremiah 29:11, God already has an "expected end" in place for all of us. He has expectations for our lives, and the truth of the matter is this; if we refuse to submit our dreams to God, we actually limit our potential for success. Why? Well, let's read the words of Ephesians 3:20: *"Now unto him that is able to do **exceeding abundantly above all that we ask or think**, according to the power that worketh in us."*

Because our dreams are mostly a collection of desires that originate in our own minds, this means that we are limited to dreaming only what we are able to think of. What we can think of is all that we can imagine, and in turn, it's all that we can attempt to achieve. However, Ephesians 3:20 lets us know that God is able to do more with our surrendered life than we are even able to think of. When we lay our dreams at the feet of God, he begins to open doors for us that we didn't even realize existed, he broadens our horizon, and he replaces our self-serving dreams with dreams and desires that please Him. Yes, some of our dreams are outstanding, but they still fall short when compared to the destiny that God has prepared for us.

So, how do your dreams and your destiny come together?

When we surrender our dreams to God's care, He is able to use us to do great things. God places the power of his Spirit within us, and utilizes our natural talents and abilities to work out his great plan for our lives. I've heard it said before that some of the best businessmen in the world are drug dealers and pimps. Sounds absurd right? Well, think about it. It is quite obvious that some of the more successful drug dealers have an innate ability to influence people. Many of them are natural-born leaders. The problem is not with the ability; the ability is God-given. The problem is found in the fact that the drug dealers refuse to submit their abilities to God for his use. They have dreams to acquire wealth just for selfish gain, while God has a destiny lined up for them that will allow them to reach millions of people as an evangelist while also becoming wealthier than they could ever imagine. When you make it obvious to God that his will is more important to you than even your dreams, you please Him greatly, and in turn, you set yourself up for great blessings.

Take a look at an exchange between Solomon, the son of King David, and God in 1 Kings 3:5-13:

"In Gibeon the LORD appeared to Solomon in a dream by night: and God said, Ask what I shall give thee. And Solomon said, Thou hast shewed unto thy servant David my father great mercy, according as he walked before thee in truth, and in righteousness, and in uprightness of heart with thee; and thou hast kept for him this great kindness, that thou hast given him a son to sit on his throne, as it is this day. And now, O LORD my God, thou hast made thy servant king instead of David my father: and I am but a little child: I know not how to go out or come in. And thy servant is in the midst of thy people which thou hast chosen, a great people that cannot be numbered nor counted for multitude. Give therefore thy servant an understanding heart to judge thy people; that I may discern between good and bad: for who is able to judge this thy so great a people? And the speech pleased the LORD, that Solomon had asked this thing. And God said unto him, Because thou hast asked this thing, and hast not asked for thyself long life; neither hast asked riches for thyself, nor hast asked the life of thine enemies; but hast asked for thyself understanding to discern judgment; Behold, I have done according to thy words: lo, I have given thee a wise and an understanding heart; so that there was none like thee before thee, neither after thee shall any arise like unto

*thee. And I have also given thee that which thou hast not
asked, both riches, and honour: so that there shall not be
any among the kings like unto thee all thy days."*

Because God made us, he knows everything there is to know about us. He knows the desires of our hearts. He knows our dreams. In this dialogue, we see Solomon laying aside his desires, and instead, acknowledging the desires of God. With an opportunity unlike any other—having someone who owns everything ask him what he wants—Solomon decides to ask for wisdom to judge the people of God properly. God is so pleased with his request, that he grants him wisdom beyond his expectations, and even gives him wealth and fame that is greater than he could have ever imagined.

Laying your agenda at the feet of God allows him to do great, unimaginable things in your life.

One thing we must remember is that whatever God is able to do in our lives is *according to the power that worketh in us*; which means that God needs our participation in order to make destiny happen for us. Romans 12:1 says for us to present ourselves to Christ as a *living sacrifice*. God needs your mind, heart, and body to accomplish His will in your life. One of my favorite verses is found in II Timothy 1:6 where Paul advises Timothy to "stir up the gift of God" that was inside of him. Paul, being a man of great insight, noticed the immensity of the gift that God had placed within Timothy, and he urged him to participate in the process of working out his destiny. To stir up your gift is to engage yourself completely in the plan of God for your life; to step out and *do*, even when you don't exactly know what to do. Just keep stirring!

It is most certainly a sacrifice to give your dreams to God and pursue the destiny that he has for you. But, God desires for your life to give him glory. It doesn't matter if your dream is to be a world renowned chef, or the President of the United States, God wants to use your life to reveal himself to the world around you. As we give ourselves to him, the power of God takes residence in our hearts, and God will use our surrendered lives to transform our dreams into destiny, and in turn, we glorify Him. A man who desires to have destiny must still be committed to the work and struggle that it takes to fulfill a dream whether you acknowledge God or not. It takes no less work for your destiny to be revealed than it takes for your dreams to become reality.

It's amazing to me how many men of God are envious of other men who fail to acknowledge God but yet are very wealthy and successful. The Bible advises us against this sort of attitude. Psalms 37:4-7 says, *"Delight thyself also in the Lord: and he shall give thee the desires of thine heart. Commit thy way unto the Lord; trust also in him; and he shall bring it to pass. And he shall bring forth thy righteousness as the light, and thy judgment as the noonday. Rest in the Lord, and wait patiently for him: fret not thyself because of him who prospereth in his way, because of the man who bringeth wicked devices to pass."*

Instead of sitting around and becoming bitter as you watch men of the world following their Godless passions and becoming wealthy, it is your call as a man of God to *commit your ways* to the Lord and follow after His passions. This does not mean that you give up on your dreams; it just means that your dreams take a backseat to the agenda of God. As you consign your dream to the care of God, and commit to the struggle of dream fulfillment, you can then trust God to *bring it to pass.*

The sad truth is that many men of God surrender their dreams to God and then stop working. Just as I said a moment ago, surrendering your dreams to God does not mean that you can now sit back in your recliner and watch God bring about destiny in your life. God forbid. It just doesn't work that way. The shame is on us for allowing the men of the world to recognize that it takes incredible effort to make a dream something more than wishful thinking; while often, we seemingly just don't get it. That's why I'll say it again; don't waste time being envious of the prosperity of those who don't acknowledge God. In all actuality, it may be time for us to take notes from them! Hard work can make things happen for you even if you don't allow God to be the head of your life, but I am determined to be successful and make God proud at the same time.

You are a man of God, and God has also made you a dreamer. The gift of being a dreamer is one that should not be taken lightly. It is my belief that God bestows the gift of dreaming upon certain men before he ever reveals to them what they ought to dream. Psalms 37:23 reminds us that the steps of a man of God are ordered by the Lord. This means that every step that you are intended to take in your life has already been thought out in the mind of God and planned to lead you into your purpose. An amazing thing happens when your steps are ordered by the Lord. You would think that having your steps laid out by God would mean that you would avoid all trouble and dire circumstances. But, many times, it's the contrary. The steps to destiny are not always traveled through a patch of sweet-smelling roses. Instead, you will still have to deal with times of adversity. However, the one thing you can rely on, is the fact that God is faithful, and if you allow Him to begin a great work in your life, he will complete that work, and bring you into the great *expected end* that he planned for you long before you entered this world.

Therefore, because God knows us best, the greatest thing that we can do with our dreams is give them to God and allow him to make them over and lead us into our preordained place of destiny. I don't know about you, but I won't have life any other way.

Chapter 10

Tips for Husbands

As I got further and further into this book, I felt like I should write a few tips for dream success that are specifically for husbands and wives.

So, as a husband, what can you do within the framework of your household to enhance your dream pursuit?

First of all, treat your wife with love and respect. This is absolutely essential to your success. 1 Peter 3:7 says, *"Husbands, must give honor to (their) wives.....treat her as you should so your prayers will not be hindered."* If you neglect your wife, treat her harshly, or refuse to honor her, your prayers aren't getting anywhere with God. I've heard some call the prayers of a husband who is not treating his wife right; "rooftop prayers." What does that mean? Well, your prayers aren't going any further than the roof of your house. God has shut you off! If you have a nonexistent prayer life, you'll have a tough time making any progress on your dream projects.

My advice to you is this: get your relationship in order (if it isn't in order already), and keep it that way. Besides, an unhappy wife makes for an unhappy home; and trying to be productive in an unhappy home is virtually impossible.

Secondly, take care of your business around the house. If your wife's car is breaking down, take it to the shop. If the dishes need to be washed, take care of it. If the grass needs to be cut, make sure it gets done. A home takes a lot of maintenance, and if you don't help out around the house, your wife is not likely to support your dream pursuits. A wife will tend to look at your dreams as "just another thing" that's causing you to leave work around the house undone.

Now, trust me; I'm no Mr. Fix-it, but I do make an effort to help clean the house, take care of household tasks, and run necessary errands. Yes, even the grocery store! Doing these things is obligatory if you want your wife to stay engaged in your dreams. Trust me; you don't want her to disengage herself. God created a wife as a helper to her husband, but when she becomes disinterested in your dream pursuits, you lose the advantage of that God-ordained help.

Lastly, while you are chasing your dreams, you have to do *something* to make some money for your household. Gentlemen; GET A JOB!

As I spoke about in chapter five, the *meantime* is a reality for all of us, and you have to handle it appropriately. First Timothy 5:8 says, *"But if any provide not for his own, and especially for those of his own house, he hath denied the faith, and is worse than an infidel."* If you are not making any money with your dream just yet, you have to get a job! No exceptions. No excuses. Your wife should not be responsible for paying all of the bills while you work solely on your dreams. You have a responsibility to provide for your family. This verse illustrates the severity of taking that responsibility lightly. It says that if you refuse to provide for your family, you are "worse than an infidel" (an unbeliever). It even states that you have "denied the faith;" which means that you have literally turned your back on following the Lord.

Now, I understand if you and your wife have a discussion and come to an understanding that you will simply work on your dream for a period of time. But, it should be common sense that you will contribute even more heavily to the work that needs to be done around the house in that case.

As men, we don't always deal very well with another man trying to tell us how to handle ourselves; and I wouldn't dare attempt to tell you how to deal with your wife. But, if you want to keep the peace in your home, you have to consider these things. I mean, your wife will not want to hear about your dream pursuit, neither will she want to support you the way you want her to if you neglect your responsibilities at home. But, can you blame her?

No matter how focused you are to chase your dreams, your first job and highest responsibility is always supposed to be taking care of your family. If you don't make your family a priority in your life, you run the risk of turning the atmosphere in your home into one that is no longer conducive to dream pursuit.

The motto of this story: Take care of your business at home before you worry about pursuing your dreams.

Another thing; tell your wife how important she is to your dream pursuit. Let her know how critical her support and encouragement is to you. It may be possible that she doesn't even realize the power that she possesses. If you tell her, she will make a purposeful effort to support you.

Now, encourage her to read the next chapter.

Chapter 11

Tips for Wives

Hello ladies, you may be wondering why your husband has asked you to read a book that is written for men. Don't worry. Although the book in its entirety *was* written for men, this chapter is for you. So, if you would be so kind, take just a few moments and read the next few pages. I believe it will help you and your husband.

First of all, let me ask you this: Are you married to a dreamer?

If your answer is anything other than, "yes," you had better pay closer attention.

YOU *ARE* MARRIED TO A DREAMER! I wrote this chapter just to remind some and inform others, that as a wife of a dreamer, you possess a great deal of power as it relates to the dreams of your husband becoming reality.

The Bible declares that God used the rib of man to form the woman. Genesis 2:21-23 says, *"And the Lord God caused a deep sleep to fall upon Adam, and he slept: and he took one of his ribs, and closed up the flesh instead thereof; And the rib, which the LORD God had taken from man, made he a woman, and brought her unto the man.*

And Adam said, this is now bone of my bones, and flesh of my flesh: she shall be called Woman, because she was taken out of Man. Therefore shall a man leave his father and his mother, and shall cleave unto his wife: and they shall be one flesh."

God formed the first wife from the rib of the first husband signifying the closeness and internal connection of the man and woman who commit to the covenant relationship of marriage. Man and wife are literally connected from the inside-out. With this level of closeness, a wife has a very unique ability to encourage her husband in ways that no one else can. You can literally build him up into victory and success or tear him down into failure and defeat. You can make him feel as if his dreams are possible, or cause him to believe that his dreams are out of reach. I remember one evening when I was feeling particularly discouraged and wondering if this book would really help anyone, my wife—out of the clear blue sky—asked me, "Hey, how is your book coming along?" Just that question alone gave me the strength that I needed to continue to write. As men, we have to feel like our wives believe with us and in us. If my wife tells me that something is possible, no one in the world can convince me that it's not possible.

With that in mind, make it a point to speak words that build your husband up. For me, there is no word of encouragement like the words that come from my wife. She is the one person whose words carry the most weight as it relates to me and the concerns of my life. Someone else could spend an hour talking to me and still not have the effect that my wife can have by simply saying, "I believe in you." As the wife of a dreamer, you must think before you speak. In times of frustration with your husband, you cannot allow yourself to fly off the handle and say things that will discourage him from pursuing his dreams. Be proactive and purposeful with every word that you speak; knowing that your words have the power to construct an atmosphere of success in your home, or an atmosphere of defeat and unbelief.

Your support is critical to your husband's success. You have to help him believe that his dream is really possible. One of the hardest things for a man to do is to continue to believe in his dreams as he deals with the mounting weight of an everyday reality staring him in the face each morning. Many times, our ego won't let us tell you how much we're struggling, but it's your support and encouragement that causes us to maintain our belief despite everything that we're looking at in our present situation. Your kind words, beautiful smile, and even a simple rub on our head means a lot to us.

Even if your husband is not doing all that he should be doing around the house, it is still not wise to destroy his dreams by your lack of support or words of defeat. First Peter 3:1 says, *"Likewise, ye wives, be in subjection to your own husbands; that, if any obey not the word, they also may without the word be won by the conversation of the wives."* Though your husband may be negligent of his duties in the home, you must try to be loving anyhow. You stand a better chance of winning him over with sweet words than nagging and complaining all of the time. Take your concerns to the Lord in silent prayer, and God will cause him to see the error of his ways. If you try to handle things on your own, you risk discouraging him to the point that he doesn't see the need to pursue his dreams any longer.

In all that you do, be wise. Ask the Lord for wisdom, and you will play a vital part in your husband achieving his dreams. You will be the source of his strength and the fuel that keeps him motivated to succeed.

Extra Tips for Dreamers

Here are just a few extra things I thought I would share with you. Maybe some of these ideas can help you.

1. Start a dream journal.

Nothing fancy; you can use your computer or simply purchase a notebook. Take notes every day including a date, and exactly what you worked on as it relates to your dream. I have found that the best thing to do is use a notebook and leave it in a very obvious place; where it can't be ignored. You will find that you will start to hold yourself accountable if you happen to go several days without having anything to write in your journal. After writing in your dream journal becomes habitual for you, you'll notice that if you don't have anything to write, you probably didn't do any work on your dream that day.

2. Consider getting a partner/s.

Some of our dreams are impossible to achieve without help. Many of the most successful entrepreneurs in the world today had help that may or may not be as visible as the face of the company, but were just as vital in making a venture possible. Don't miss out on your dream just because you're selfish. Talk to people. Find out who has a talent or skill that you need to make your dream a reality. It may be the case that you have a skill that they were looking for. Remember, your steps are ordered by the Lord.

3. Set up a timeline to chart your progress.

If you don't remember anything else that you have read in this book, remember this: You have to extract your dream from your mind, and make it a part of your tangible life. In other words, your dream has to cease from being simply a figment of your imagination and instead, become something that you can touch. With that in mind, *set up a timeline with goals and checkpoints to chart your progress toward dream fulfillment.* You can start out with five short-term goals, and as you complete each goal, check it off of your sheet until you have every one completed. Then, write new goals, and repeat the process.

One of the hardest things to deal with as a dreamer is the feeling of not making any progress even when you are trying very hard to make things happen. This technique of writing short-term goals and checking them off as they are completed can be extremely helpful, as you will be able to see your progress in bold black and white.

4. Establish a dream relationship.

It was about a year ago when I realized that I needed to find another way to look at my dreams. The more I thought about it, it became apparent to me that I needed to actually develop a *relationship* with my dreams. I know, I know, that's sort of weird, but hear me out.

In any relationship, there are several components that must exist in order for that union to be successful. Here are a few things to think about as you consider establishing your own dream relationship:

+ ***Desire***

First of all, you have to understand how much you *desire* to have the relationship. This will determine the effort and amount of *sweat equity* you are willing to invest in sustaining it. You may be thinking that sweat equity doesn't apply to relationships, but I believe it most definitely does. Any relationship that you are not willing to work on is a relationship that is bound to fail. In much the same way, if your desire to accomplish your dream is not very significant, you won't be willing to invest the long hours and sleepless nights that it takes to see a dream come to life.

+ ***Commitment***

Are you committed to the relationship? As I mentioned in an earlier chapter, commitment is necessary to the pursuit of your dream. In the same way that you are committed to any other relationship that is important to you, you have to be committed to your dream relationship if you expect it to render results to you. If you are not committed, I mean totally committed to this relationship, it will fall apart. You will find yourself placing your dream near or at the bottom of your priorities; and as we all know, if a relationship is not a priority for you, it's one that has little chance of flourishing. A relationship that lacks commitment won't last because, quite frankly, it's a relationship that you don't really care about. You can't possibly care about a relationship if you refuse to commit to it. It's simple as that.

* *Fidelity*

Can your dream depend on you? Are you faithful to your dream, or is this a one-sided relationship? Your dream will always be there urging you to make a move; encouraging you to step out of the box. Are you a reliable partner, or is your dream wondering where you've been? If your dream has to stay up late at night by the phone, waiting on you to call, you are not showing yourself to be faithful in your dream relationship. Being faithful in your dream relationship means you won't lie to your dream and tell it that you're going to do something and continually fail to do what you said you were going to do.

Ask yourself; *can my dream trust me?*

As I started looking at my dream pursuit as an actual relationship, I began to take my dreams a lot more seriously. I have never been the type of person who wants to disappoint the people who depend on me, and in the same way, I don't want to disappoint my dream. I realize that my dream is counting on me, and I'm determined to do everything that I can to make sure I create a successful partnership that is progressing toward a common goal.

No matter what; all the tips and techniques, words of advice or encouragement in the world won't work for you if you're not willing to work yourself. Your dream is ultimately your responsibility. Just like a jump shot or a golf swing, the possibility of success is determined by your follow-through. The bottom-line is this: if you are a dreamer, you have to *do something* about your dream. Stop sitting around. Stop hoping for change. Get up and do something. You may feel like you don't have the resources to make your dream happen, but that's not true. Look at it like this; everyone is on a different level. Some have degrees, some don't. Some have lots of money, others don't. However, no matter what level you are on, there is a way to get to the next level. You just have to do what you can with the level you are currently on. You may not be able to do with your dream what others can do with theirs at this time, but there is always *something* that you can do, and something is always better than nothing. As I stated before, don't allow *anything* to become an excuse. Instead, look at every obstacle as just another challenge that you must overcome, and eventually, you will begin to see your dreams unfold right before your eyes.

It's time for those men who allow themselves to dream to begin to put in the work that it takes to see their dreams become reality. I don't know how you feel, but I'm ready to make it happen!

Epilogue

Dream pursuit that pleases God has to be a faith thing. The bible declares that "without faith it is impossible to please (God)." So, as you strive to achieve your dreams you must never forget that faith is always the key component; faith in God, not solely in your own abilities.

Just a few months ago, I had a dream that was rather peculiar. In the dream, I was standing on a small block in the middle of the air. All around me was darkness. It appeared that if I stepped in any direction, I would fall into a bottomless pit. For a long period of time, I just stood there, afraid to move. Then, from out of nowhere, I heard a voice.

"Step forward."

"How?" I asked hesitantly.

"Step forward."

By this time, I was looking around and wondering how I could possibly take a step without falling into what looked like a never-ending abyss. The voice spoke again.

"Step....forward."

With my heart pounding as if it was going to jump right out of my chest, I stepped forward, and let out a scream, "Ahhh!!"

I just knew I was headed for destruction.

But, to my surprise, another platform appeared underneath my feet. I stood there in amazement for a few moments, then I stepped forward again, and amazingly, another platform appeared in the utter darkness.

After I woke up, that dream stayed on my mind for the entire day. But it wasn't until a few days later, in a quiet moment with God, that the Spirit of God began to reveal to me exactly what the dream meant.

In the dream, I was standing in complete darkness in the middle of the air. The block that I was standing on was very small. This signified how I felt about my present situation. When I looked around in my present real-life state, all I saw was mounting bills and uncertainty. The opportunities around me, much like the block I stood on in my dream, seemed to be very limited. How could I possibly believe that God has great things in store for me?

For God to tell me to step off of the block and into the darkness around me seemed absurd; but, what He was trying to show me is that I have to trust that He knows how to make something out of nothing. Although I couldn't see how it would work, if I had the faith to step out, God would make everything work out for my good.

God said to me, "If you will simply begin to walk toward what I have for you, even though you don't see anything but darkness in front of you, I will begin to build your destiny around you; right before your eyes."

Then, it all clicked. God was trying to show me that I needed to learn to walk by faith. When you walk by faith, you don't see how everything is going to work out, but you keep walking. All I needed in my dream was enough faith to keep walking. All I needed was enough faith for the very next step. That's all you need, too. Don't worry about step #2 or #3. Just have enough faith to take step #1.

Walking is a verb; which means it is an action word. It's something that you must do. It takes faith to please God with your dream pursuit. But, you must decide to start walking if you want something to happen in your life.

So, go ahead, take that first step. Don't be afraid of the darkness around you. If you commit to the first step, God will show you how to take the next step.

Do you have enough faith to listen to God and allow Him to build something great around you?

I'm determined to walk. What about you?

Acknowledgments

First and foremost, I have to thank **God** for giving me the drive to write and constraining me to complete this book. I am so *grateful* that God loves me like he does. Lord, I'm honored to take this journey with you. This is only the beginning!

Much of the credit for this book goes to my wife, **La'Shon.** Baby, you are an awesome woman. I love you more than anything. Thanks for not becoming annoyed with all of the questions that I asked about my book. Your feedback was extremely helpful and necessary. Also, thanks for blessing me with such beautiful kids. *Tike* and *Maddie*, Daddy loves ya'll! Get ready for an extraordinary ride!

To my parents, Michael and Patricia Ford, I would be *nothing* without you. Thanks for putting up with all of my mess as a young man and still loving me. Thanks for contributing your money and time. Thanks for believing in my dreams with me. If God would have given me the option, I couldn't have prayed for better parents. I love you both more than I can explain in words.

I have to thank God for giving me such great siblings. To Patrick, Patrice (Deep), and Ebony: You guys are the best! Thanks for just being *you.*

To my in-laws, Eugene and Linda Reid: thanks for your support, and thanks for making my *wife!* You all have been a source of support every since I first met you. I love you guys!

I believe I have the greatest pastor in the world—hands down. Pastor Hurley J. Coleman Jr. has been a pillar in my life for several years now. Pastor, thanks for writing the foreword for this book. I have learned so much under your ministry (as if you didn't notice by how many times I quoted you in this book!). Thanks for simply being *real.*

First Lady Sandra Coleman; thanks for your moral support and prayers. You have helped me in more ways than you know. Whenever I have needed an *encouraging* word, it seems that you always know what to say.

To my extended family; aunts, uncles, cousins, and everyone in between, thanks for every word of encouragement and every bit of *love* that you've shown me. I can't name all of you, but I love you all. I'm so glad to be a part of such a crazy family!

Special thanks to my friends and family at the World Outreach Campus in Saginaw, MI, my best friend, Warren Franklin—thanks for being a listening ear, and the staff at AuthorHouse for putting together a *wonderful* presentation of my work.

If I missed calling your name, charge it to my mind and not my *heart.* I'll catch you in the next one!

Much Love,

Michael Ford II

Contact Michael

Visit Michael's official website at
www.michaelfordii.com for events, to request a
speaking engagement, or to simply keep in touch.

Email: info@michaelfordii.com

Follow Michael on Twitter! www.twitter.com/gggceo